PRENTICE-HALL FOUNDATIONS OF EDUCATION SERIES
Hobert W. Burns, Editor

FOUNDATIONS OF EDUCATION SERIES

THOMAS E. CLAYTON

PRENTICE-HALL, INC., ENGLEWOOD CLIFFS, N. J.

TEACHING AND LEARNING
A Psychological Perspective

PRENTICE-HALL INTERNATIONAL, INC., *London*
PRENTICE-HALL OF AUSTRALIA, PTY., LTD., *Sydney*
PRENTICE-HALL OF CANADA, LTD., *Toronto*
PRENTICE-HALL OF INDIA (PRIVATE) LTD., *New Delhi*
PRENTICE-HALL OF JAPAN, INC., *Tokyo*

FOUNDATIONS OF EDUCATION SERIES
TEACHING AND LEARNING:
A PSYCHOLOGICAL PERSPECTIVE
BY THOMAS E. CLAYTON

Library of Congress
Catalog Card No.: 65-11326

PRINTED IN THE UNITED STATES OF AMERICA
C–89402-c   C–89401-P

Public education is the "growth industry" of the nation today. Next to defense, education is the single largest enterprise in our political economy and, unlike even defense, it is the American activity that in some way or at some time directly involves every single citizen.

If public education is quantitatively important, then the training of teachers is one of the most qualitatively important undertakings of the entire educational enterprise. Indeed, the training of teachers is already the single largest undertaking of American higher education, since more college graduates enter the profession of teaching than any other vocation, and it may well be the most important undertaking of our colleges and universities.

Even so, despite the size of the American educational establishment, it is remarkable how little is understood of the educative process, especially of the intellectual bases of education that support all pedagogy; and of all those who have—in the language of defense rather than education—a "need to know," the prospective teacher has the greatest need.

Prospective teachers need to understand education through the historical perspective of Western culture—and so the series includes a volume in the history of education, a volume that may fairly be called an intellectual history of education, rather than a mere chronology of educationally important dates or historically important pedagogues.

Prospective teachers need to understand that the school, and the children and teachers in it, are social organisms inevitably influenced by the nature of the society in which they exist—and so the series includes a volume in the sociology of education, a volume showing how the public school reflects, for better or worse, the reality rather than the image of contemporary American society.

Prospective teachers need to understand the psychological nature of children and how it limits, if not determines, what schools should or should not do (Is it reasonable to expect, as many teachers do, a six- or seven-year-old to sit quietly and attentively for a major portion of his waking day?)—and so the series includes a volume in the psychology of education, a volume that pays particular attention to the ways in which children grow, develop, mature, learn, and change their behavior.

FOUNDATIONS OF EDUCATION SERIES

Prospective teachers need to understand the close functional relationship between philosophy and practice in education and, at the same time, to see that many of the practical problems they will face as teachers (e.g., How shall I grade? Shall I use drill? Should children be segregated on such bases as talent, color, or religion?) are solvable only in terms of prior philosophic inquiry—and so the series includes a volume in philosophy of education, a volume that views philosophy as dressed in the working clothes of a practical discipline rather than in the formal attire of impractical abstractions.

Prospective teachers need perspective to see the historical, philosophical, social, and psychological foundations of education in a context both different and larger than any one locality, region, or nation affords—and so the series includes a volume in comparative education, a volume designed to help the teacher compare and contrast his experience and educational system with the experiences and systems of other teachers in other nations and cultures.

These things the prospective teacher needs to know; he needs to be well grounded in the foundations of education, for they represent the intellectual tools that can give him scholarly leverage in his profession. But, given the thinness of time and the immensity of need in teacher education curriculums, how is this to be done?

The authors of this series believe that no single volume, be it a large, well-edited book of readings or a long treatise by one scholar, can meet the challenge of offering prospective teachers what they need to know as well as can a series of smaller volumes, each written by a specialist in one particular aspect of the foundations of education. Each volume in this series, by design, can stand alone as an introduction to an intellectual discipline; but when taken together the volumes unite these independent yet related disciplines into a series that offers prospective teachers a fuller, more unified introduction to the subject matters that underlie the profession of teaching.

We are convinced that prospective teachers who study these volumes in the foundations of education, and who discuss the concepts and issues presented with their instructors, will take to their future classrooms a firmer understanding not only of how to do the teaching job at hand but, more significant, of why their teaching job is so surpassingly important.

Hobert W. Burns

This book was conceived as an attempt to examine and apply the materials and ideas from psychology and related fields that might be most helpful to teachers—prospective and practicing—in illuminating an understanding of the teaching-learning process. This selection and treatment of topics reflects the author's own interests and beliefs, as well as his perceptions—over a number of years—of the apparent interests and reactions of classes of prospective teachers.

This is neither an introductory psychology text nor a survey of the field of educational psychology. It does not attempt to reflect current research emphasis in the field. Technical terminology has not been used for its own sake. The terminology used is that which seems most likely to explicate the ideas under consideration. Many conventional topics in educational psychology have been omitted, and much conventional terminology has been avoided.

Students who are interested in or have need of the study of psychology or educational theory, as such, must go beyond this volume. It is hoped that the annotated bibliography at the end of each Part will be helpful in directing beginning explorations in these disciplines. In this book, only some of the foundations of education are exposed.

Many books in educational psychology start with the learner, logically move to the learning process, and conclude with some material on teachers and teaching. That conventional organization is here reversed because of the conviction that, psychologically, prospective teachers are likely to be concerned first with teaching, next with the learning process that teaching is supposed to direct, and finally with the nature of the organism doing the learning. Those who wish to change this order in their reading are invited to do so.

Part I expresses a current concern for an analysis of the teaching process and the behavior of teachers in the process. This is a relatively recent emphasis in educational psychology, and one that is long overdue. Part II outlines a general point of view about the learning process, gives some historical and theoretical perspectives that should enhance an attempt to build an understanding of learning as a process, and presents a summation of empirical findings about learning. Part III uses two broad theoretical models as a framework to establish an understanding of the probable behavior of the learner; it concludes with a specific topic, intelli-

PREFACE

gence, which is a fundamental example of one aspect of the learning individual.

It is postulated that psychological understandings can illuminate the teaching function and, thus, affect the eventual behavior of teachers.

Thomas E. Clayton

ix

CONTENTS

PART ONE THE TEACHING PROCESS
FROM A PSYCHOLOGICAL POINT OF VIEW

Everyone seems to know the answer. Most people in American society have been exposed to some twelve or more years of "education" in "school" where "teaching" has been a daily occurrence.

Recently, some college students planning to become teachers were asked to write their answers to the question, "What is teaching?" Their responses, difficult to classify, stated that teaching is "the passing of facts, ideas, and part of yourself to others . . . the communication of factual and interpretive knowledge between teacher and student."

Many responses followed this view of the transmission of factual and interpretive knowledge by one person (the teacher) to another (the taught). Some went a little beyond this to say that teaching is "the skill of imparting knowledge to students in a manner likely to stimulate their interest and retention . . . a communication between two or more people in which one of the persons involved learns something from another . . . a practice associated mainly with school where people who have been previously educated try to teach children academics . . . an activity involved with everyday life."

3

TEACHING AND PSYCHOLOGICAL UNDERSTANDING

1

Some comments stressed the goals of teaching as "teaching skills in learning, encouraging learning, and providing guidance to formulations of standards and ideals on which to base a life . . . teaching children what we already know or acquired through school, teaching them how to be useful in life and to become good citizens of the state . . . preparing young men and women to participate successfully in their society."

Some focussed on the children and their development, describing teaching as "cultivating the minds of children, stimulating them and causing their minds to be filled with the thousands of things that make the world what it is, and giving children understanding of the world in which they live and some means of coping with this world . . . inspiring a child's will to learn and directing this will in the paths that will be most beneficial to him throughout his life, whether it be for business or pleasure."

Some responses, concentrating on the teacher as a person with a mission, stated that teaching is "a gift given to a certain few for the purpose of helping and educating others to grow to their fullest capacities as persons . . . a challenge placed upon an individual . . . a dedicated position in which one desires to educate the future generations of America."

Finally, a response that is more modest in tone, but more comprehensive in statement, professed that "there is no adequate definition of teaching; however, it does encompass the following ideas: leading youngsters to develop a desire to learn; having a dedication to learning and passing this on; being aware of the needs of children and helping them grow in meeting these needs; being able to know where to turn for concrete information and how to communicate this in an effective manner; and acting as a catalyst in developing ideas."

Though the psychologist or the professional educator may not agree with some of the concepts implied in these statements, they indicate the picture of teaching these young people developed during their years of schooling. Only recently has there been much of a concerted attempt to conceptualize the roles of teachers or to develop an analytical framework for describing the job of teaching. Obviously, teaching is what teachers do. They do many things. They present information orally; they give instructions to pupils; they organize materials for pupils to deal with. They have goals, worries, fears, frustrations, and satisfactions related to their jobs. They react emotionally to pupils and other teachers. They estimate the progress of pupils. They carry out a variety of activities that are characteristic of the institution we call "the school." All of these things are part of teaching.

ROLES OF TEACHERS

One of the recent analyses of the roles of teachers suggests six roles, organized into three categories (4).[1] The first category includes the role of the teacher as a director of learning (emphasizing working with groups), and the teacher's role as a counselor or guidance worker (emphasizing

[1] Numbers in parentheses refer to selections in the bibliography at the end of the Part in which the reference occurs.

concern with the individual). These roles are seen as promoting pupil growth. The liaison roles of the teacher include the third role, the teacher as mediator of the culture, and the fourth role, the teacher as a link with the community. Finally, the program-building roles include the teacher's fifth role, that of a member of the school staff and his sixth role, that of a member of the profession. All of these roles and their related activities can be included as part of the definition of teaching.

If we look at teaching from various points of view, we will find that teaching can be described *historically* in terms of the developing activities and expectations of teachers over a period of time. It can be described *comparatively* in terms of the status and activities of the teacher in various cultures and national systems. It can be described *philosophically* in terms of various systems of belief, understanding, and analysis. It can be described *sociologically* in terms of the particular purposes, values, institutions, and common behavior of a particular culture. Or it can be described *psychologically*.

PSYCHOLOGY AND TEACHING

In this volume, we are concerned with the psychological description of teaching and some of its implications. Since psychology is the study of the behavior of organisms, we are concerned in teaching with the behavior of the teacher, the behavior of those who are taught, and the relationship between the two. This concern might include nonhuman animals, and frequently does. In this volume, however, nonhuman animals will be dealt with only as they throw light on the behavior of humans. We are not so much concerned with the school as an institution, the organization of groups, political pressures, or the administration of schools. We may become concerned with these things insofar as they affect the behavior of individual teachers and as this behavior influences the learning of pupils. If so, we are concerned with them as influences, but not necessarily in their own right.

Psychologically, teaching may be considered the processes and activities of organisms involved in directing the learning process. Those things that facilitate (or hinder), clarify (or confuse) this process are our legitimate areas of inquiry.

Psychologically, what does it mean to be a director of a learning process? It means that one must perform certain activities, behave in certain ways, and influence others in particular directions in order that they will come out of the situation different from the way they were before or from the way they would have been without the teacher's influence.

To what extent can such a process be predicted in definite terms? To what extent does "directing" the learning process imply control? Can we predict the specific results a teacher's behavior will produce in his pupils' behavior? To what extent can the learning process be under the "direction" of the teacher? Much of this volume will be directed to attempting answers to these questions.

5

It is my contention that (at our present stage of development) teaching is more art than science or technology. Like any artist, the teacher's main function is creative decision-making about how to act, what to do, and how to perform in order to achieve the results he desires. The teacher desires changes in his pupils' behavior that will better fit them to take their place in the world the teacher perceives as important. At the present time, there is no complete catalogue of recipes to combine certain ingredients under certain conditions to obtain certain effects. If there were, teaching would be technology, and we could train teachers to apply purely technical skills to prearranged objectives. Similarly, there are too many unknowns—too many uncontrolled variables in the teaching process—for it to be the kind of situation we conventionally think of as "scientific." Too much of teaching is still necessarily spontaneous reaction to immediate situations to have it fall under the rubrics of modern science.

Hence, the intuitive responses, the selection of patterns according to taste, the variability in desired outcomes, and the variability in actual outcomes, all of which are more characteristic of art than science or technology are equally characteristic of teaching.

To follow this analogy further, we have only to look at teachers in action. Many of us can think of the rare teacher who is a magnificent "primitive," whose use of the media of teaching is appropriate and effective, who relates to pupils in such a way that they respond positively, who seems to know what subject matter will achieve the right effects at a particular time, who relates to colleagues in ways that will enhance the total educational program, and whose evaluation of pupils' progress is shrewd, fair, and enlightening. We can conceive of this teacher producing masterpieces of pupil growth without a background in psychology, without rational analysis of the psychological factors involved in the process. We can even concede that such rational analysis might interfere with the performance. However, such a "Grandma Moses" is rare.

It is much easier to think of primitives who turn out pitiful products, who create more problems in the teaching process than they solve, whose stock of technique is so limited that they have no resources at hand, whose lack of understanding of the psychology underlying teaching is so great that they are unable to make corrections or revisions in their work.

It is possible to think of the opposite extreme, the person whose understanding of the science underlying the art is sound, well organized, and easily verbalized, but whose teaching performance fails to apply these understandings. There is a gap somewhere between the recognition of a principle, which comes from science, and its application in an artistic performance. There is always hope that this person can improve if helped to analyze his performance in the light of existing knowledge and if encouraged to use a scientific process as well as knowledge in evaluating and revising his work. He may not become the master teacher, but he may become a competent craftsman who turns out acceptable products in an acceptable way.

We can also think of the person who fits the current professional image of the master teacher. This person has a philosophical point of view and a value system that permits choices of appropriate objectives in teaching. He understands the society in which he lives and the place of the educational process in that society. He has the historical perspective that permits him to see his work in a realistic context. He understands the background and goals of his profession. Psychologically, he understands himself, his colleagues, his pupils, and the learning process well enough to use these understandings in the teaching process. He is well acquainted with the technology of teaching and has a repertory of possible activities available. He has control of appropriate subject matter and he can select the right ideas and information to move pupils toward appropriate objectives. Above all, he is able to put these understandings and skills together in an effective performance and he can use his understanding to evaluate and improve his performance. He is what we might call a rational artist or a disciplined professional.

Most of us, as teachers, fall somewhere between these various extremes. We do some things that are effective and some that are ineffective. We have some understanding of the rationale for what we do and are able to use it for improvement, and we have some gaps in our understanding and are puzzled about procedures that do not work well. We have a relatively limited repertory of technical skills and we tend to use only a portion of the available technological aids. Our decision-making varies from an intuitive response to a carefully planned series of activities. There are times when we know we have done a poor job and times when we have the glow of satisfaction achieved by the artist who has turned out a product or a performance that is right.

7

THE CONTEXT OF TEACHING

Learning goes on in many ways and under many circumstances. From one point of view, learning is contiguous with living and goes on in all circumstances.

The word teaching is used more restrictively. It is possible to conceive of teaching as going on without a living teacher as in the phrase, "Experience is the best teacher." It is probably more useful for our purposes to think of teaching as involving a person in a teaching role. In that sense, each of us in our lifetime has many teachers—parents, other adults, friends, peers, colleagues, public figures, bosses, and teachers in schools. Most of us are teachers in the sense that we sometimes work with others to get them to change their ways of behaving. In some societies, the organization of the teaching function is quite casual or informal; in others, complex institutions with the major function of teaching are developed. It is possible to organize teaching functions in vastly different ways.

In the United States (and many similar societies), there are probably three major institutions that share the basic teaching functions: the home, the peer group, and the school. Tremendously significant teaching is done by the first two, although somewhat informally and with less conscious concern about "teaching." We must deal with these institutions, especially as we look at the basic pattern of human growth and development in our culture. More formally and consciously, we tend to think of the school as the institution officially charged with carrying out teaching processes, and the teacher in the school as the person who primarily bears the title of "teacher."

THE AMERICAN SCHOOL

The American school is an extremely complex institution with organizational patterns, ways of working, common practices, and customs, which tend to define the context in which formal teaching goes on. There are many differences among individual schools. Certain differences separate public schools and nonpublic schools. There are regional differences that affect the operation of schools, and there are customs that separate the typical elementary school from the high school. It is probably improper to talk about "the American school" in any detail, and more useful to talk about individual schools and specific practices. Yet, there is a general pattern in American educational institutions and much of our thinking about teaching is channelled by this context. It will be difficult as we analyze teaching and learning to distinguish between the basic principles involved in these processes, the common practices in our schools, and the particular image of school practices we have derived from our individual experiences. We will try to be as clear as possible in making these distinctions.

It is probably important to recognize that the school as an institution and education as a social enterprise are involved in activities other than teaching, and are subject to pressures that hinder a sound teaching process. As we look more carefully at teaching, learning, and human behavior, it will become clear that the psychology of teaching is only one aspect of the totality of teaching. The reader must explore all aspects of the teaching process in order to maintain a meaningful perspective.

PSYCHOLOGICAL UNDERSTANDINGS

It is a common experience for persons who are identified as psychologists to encounter a rather strange reaction from laymen in social situations. The lady at the cocktail party who says coyly, "Now don't you analyze me!" illustrates this reaction. (The person who is identified as a teacher is also likely to get a different, but equally unwarranted reaction.) Concerning the psychologist, there seems to be the rather flattering assumption of the existence of esoteric knowledge and skills and the rather unflattering ascription of some quality of black magic to these skills. Fortunately, or unfortunately, a knowledge of or concern with psychology does not confer such power.

However, like any branch of knowledge, psychology does have a contribution to make in deepening understanding, providing some tools of analysis, offering a conceptual framework to improve our ways of thinking, and illuminating an area of everyday life and work. Except in limited cases, it does not give specific "how to do it" answers to major life problems. As in most disciplines, understanding is the intervening variable between the existing knowledge and its specific application. It may be a long road between a psychological understanding of an aspect of the learning process and its translation by the teacher into specific classroom behavior with a predictable result in the behavior of the learner. This road can only be travelled by the teacher himself. In this book, the best we can do is to deal with the concepts and information from the field of psychology that are most likely to contribute to understandings that may be helpful to the teacher, and to try to point out where some of the roads may lead from there.

PSYCHOLOGY AND COMMON SENSE

Another common reaction to contact with psychological knowledge is, "It's only common sense." It is not always easy to distinguish between common sense and uncommon sense. Certain common-sense understandings of human behavior do prove to be true when subjected to psychological scrutiny. Others turn out to be utter nonsense. It is obviously common sense, at least in our culture, that a child who misbehaves (whatever that means) should be punished. Psychology would ask, "Under what conditions will what kind of punishment result in what kind of change in behavior?" or, even more appropriately, "Under what conditions will what kind of *treatment* result in what kind of change?" The result of such an investigation would indicate that some aspects of the common-sense approach are sound, others quite unsound.

It is true that, in initial contact with a field of study or an activity, we must rely on common sense to get started. In as complex an activity as teaching, reasonable analysis on a common-sense level is still necessary, though not sufficient, as a way of guiding practices. Yet common sense alone is too spotty, too contradictory, and too biased to be an adequate basis for understanding and applying the teaching process. One of the contributions of a field of investigation like psychology is its organization and coding of certain aspects of common sense into a consistent and coordinated pattern that may be applicable to common pursuits. In this process, other aspects of "common sense" will be found to be neither commonly applicable nor sensible.

PSYCHOLOGICAL KNOWLEDGE AND PSYCHOLOGICAL FASHION

In the long history of man's systematic study of the phenomena of the world around him, the development of a science of psychology is relatively recent. Any systematic accretion of psychological knowledge scarcely goes back before the beginning of the present century. Its development on both the scholarly and the popular level has been rapid and is still continuing rapidly. There have undoubtedly been excessive premature attempts to apply partial psychological knowledge to practical human affairs. From

9

time to time, limited knowledge has been overgeneralized and applied in situations where it was not appropriate. This tendency is always a danger in a young science that has popular appeal and potential usefulness.

Dealing as they do with the whole range of the functional behavior of organisms, psychologists deal with a vast field and follow varied interests. A particular psychologist may spend most of his professional career on one aspect of the learning process or on an investigation in depth of one limited area of child growth and development. At any one time, various investigations may not appear to fit together. The knowledge of one phase may far outrun that of a related problem, or a limited principle may be seen as generally applicable. At the same time, a particular area may dominate the interest of many scholars or may catch the public fancy. During this process, a solid body of information and theory is growing to become part of the accepted fabric of psychology.

This process may also result in the temporary ascendancy of a point of view or the development of a particular set of recipes for dealing with everyday problems. Psychological fashions develop, which are related to but not totally characteristic of the entire field of psychology from which they come. After the fashion has existed for a while, its inadequacies, excesses, or limitations are felt. It may be reversed, modified, or replaced by a new fashion developed in the same way.

Examples may be given from recommended patterns of child rearing. The relatively early and limited work of Watson and others in the 1920's emphasized the principle of habit development and underemphasized the importance of internal needs and developmental processes (14). This resulted in prescriptions for child training and control of overt behavior that held for some time. Continued study of children demonstrated the inadequacies of this point of view and eventually gave rise to prescriptions that, today, seem to have been lacking in necessary controls. Permissiveness and "let the child express himself" became common prescriptions. A later fashion stressed the expression and acceptance of emotions coupled with the control of overt behavior (2). During all this time, the body of knowledge concerning the actual facts about child growth and development was growing, and more complete theoretical systems were being constructed. Similar examples could be given of school practices, based upon partial understandings of the learning process.

The practical consequences of such psychological fashions are unfortunate. The acceptance by teachers and the public of systematic theory and a solid body of knowledge suffers as a result of prescriptions based on incomplete understanding. We repeat that the road from understanding to sound application is long and full of pitfalls.

THE USES OF UNDERSTANDING

In Part Two of this volume, a point of view will be developed that perceives the result of learning as a change in the person himself. In that sense, an understanding of the psychology basic to the teaching process can help the teacher be a person different from what he would be without that understanding. He will act and react in the classroom in a manner that includes his understandings and is partially the result of his background knowledge and what it has done to him as a person.

THE SOURCES OF PSYCHOLOGICAL UNDERSTANDING

The two branches of psychology that contribute most directly to an understanding of the teaching process are the psychology of learning and the psychology of human growth and development. There is no sharp demarcation of these two areas. They, in turn, draw from other branches, which are sometimes seen as having some independent domains. These other areas include personality theory, clinical psychology, mental hygiene, social psychology, and certain aspects of psychiatry. Statistical theory and techniques contribute to all of these. Measurement and evaluation, as an organized area, contribute directly to many aspects of the teaching process. Another area that provides both undertanding and immediate application is defined as counseling and guidance. To relate psychology and education we must draw on all of these fields.

In a book of this size, we cannot deal exhaustively with all aspects of such a large field. Selection will be made of those principles, ideas, theories, techniques, and information that have the greatest probability of being applied to and of contributing understanding of the teaching process.

11

The fame of a teacher is fleeting. Mark Hopkins is best known today as the name of a noted hotel in San Francisco. Yet, as a nineteenth century thinker and teacher, he inspired a remark attributed to President James Garfield, "Only a simple bench—Mark Hopkins on one end and I on the other—and you may have all the buildings, apparatus, and libraries without him." In some ways this is a remarkable tribute to a teacher and emphasizes the importance of the teacher as person in the teaching-learning process. The metamorphosis of this phrase to its more common form, "a student on one end of a log and Mark Hopkins on the other," is curious. Yet, this change emphasizes the use of the quotation to imply that the impedimenta of modern schools are not particularly important and that a personal contact between a student and a gifted teacher is really all that is necessary. It further carries the implication that good teaching is a relatively simple process. As we consider this proposition in its second form, we are likely to start wondering what Mark Hopkins is doing and what the student is doing. Presumably, they are not just sitting there. We might further wonder how long they have been sitting there and how long they intend to continue sitting. In all probability, some verbal behavior is going on, perhaps some

INSTRUCTIONAL ACTIVITIES OF THE TEACHER

2

unverbalized behavior that might be called thinking, and perhaps certain emotional reactions; also, they may both be practicing the skills of log or bench sitting. When they leave the log or bench, they may do something that is an outcome of their having sat there. Any learning that takes place is partly the result of who Mark Hopkins is and what he has done. It also depends upon the antecedent development of the student.

Any teaching situation has antecedents in the teacher and students; it involves the teacher and students doing something, and it involves outcomes. As we deal with the learning process later in this volume, we will focus primarily on the individual learner and his behavior; however, as we look at contemporary teaching, we typically think of a group situation. The teacher usually deals with a number of students in any lengthy segment of time. Unless otherwise specified, the discussion here will assume a teacher with a group of students.

A MODEL OF THE TEACHING PROCESS

In any comprehensive or long-range teaching process we might set up the following model of the teacher's activities.

1. Identifies the expected outcomes of the process.
2. Analyzes the student and makes decisions about the student's present stage of learning.
3. Specifies the objectives of teaching in the light of the first activities.
4. Selects information and materials and makes decisions about methods.
5. Involves the student in activities presumed to lead to learning.
6. Directs and guides the learning activities.
7. Provides situations for using the learnings involved.
8. Evaluates the outcomes of the process.

In actual practice, the process is usually not this systematic and orderly. Certainly, it is not this sequential. A number of these activities may go on concurrently, earlier decisions are revised, blind alleys may cause the teacher to back up, and some degree of evaluation goes on throughout the process. Some teachers plunge into the middle and circulate through the other activities as the need is perceived.

For many teachers, little of this model is followed consciously. Many of the activities are represented by default rather than by planning. A teacher often "identifies the expected outcome" by predeciding the material to be covered and assuming that the students will "learn" the material without ever thinking through what is meant by learning the material. Teachers often "analyze" the students and make decisions about readiness simply by assuming certain common and average characteristics of the group. Information and materials are often selected by using prescribed textbooks and syllabi, and methods are frequently selected on the basis of tradition or previous unanalyzed experience.

Let us look at each point of the model to see its possible range of behavior and draw some implications about possible levels of quality in teaching. The contention here is that some level of each activity takes place whether or not the teacher plans it or is aware of it.

THE TEACHER IDENTIFIES THE EXPECTED OUTCOMES
OF THE PROCESS

One way of classifying outcomes is to consider the behavior of the learner as open to potential change in three dimensions: the cognitive, the affective, and the active. To say this another way—changes in his thinking, his feeling, and his doing. The actual outcomes will probably be a blend of all three (3).

Cognitive outcomes. The expected outcomes may be purely cognitive. The teacher may want the students to know more, to have more information, to develop concepts that are new to them, to recognize things that were previously unknown, to be able to recall information presented in the class. He may want the students to increase the complexity of their understandings, to expand existing concepts into wider ramifications, to understand more of the implications of a topic. He may want changes to occur in their modes of thinking—to have the students become more imaginative and to think more analytically, critically, or creatively.

Cognitive outcomes will vary tremendously in depth and complexity, ranging from simple recognition or recall to thorough understanding of a topic with advanced creative thinking about it. The simple statement, "Christopher Columbus discovered America in 1492," may mean only what it says: somebody named Christopher Columbus found a place called America in a year called 1492. At the simplest level, this phrase would be available for recognition or recall under appropriate stimulation, or the phrase, if repeated, would bring a stir of recognition. This cognitive outcome might be all the teacher wishes.

At a more advanced level of meaning, the phrase could stand for: Over 450 years ago at the height of the Italian Renaissance, the period of such people as Machiavelli and da Vinci, a man from Genoa, whose name has now been anglicized to "Christopher Columbus," sailed with a fleet of three ships to discover a western route to India. The voyage was financed by the Spanish throne. He landed in the region now known as the West Indies and is commonly credited with "discovering" America, although he probably did not set foot on the continents of North or South America on that first voyage.

The phrase might start many kinds of thinking—from visual recall of Renaissance paintings through the economics of the Age of Discovery to space flight in the current age. All of these thoughts and many more could be outcomes of planning to deal with Columbus.

Affective outcomes. The affective outcomes have to do with the ways the pupils feel, their emotional reactions and motivational trends. As an outcome of the teaching process, how do we want pupils to feel about music, art, or arithmetic? What kind of emotional responses do we want concerning concepts of patriotism, scientific methods, literature, or sports? How do we expect them to feel about themselves and others, and about their relationships with others? What about a feeling of pride in achievement versus modesty about accomplishments? Do we want them to enjoy or dislike intellectual pursuits? These questions of attitudes and appreciation belong to the realm of identifying expected affective outcomes.

In the Christopher Columbus example, inspection of the affective domain raises questions about the student's feelings. Is he excited, interested, bored, or disgusted about the historical material or the ideas considered? What feelings about discovery, monarchy, the Renaissance, and Columbus are generated? How will these particular feelings affect later contacts with history or attitudes toward historical events? Is an interest generated in the Renaissance and the Age of Discovery that will affect aesthetic responses toward Renaissance art or an emotional readiness to explore other periods of history? Does the particular teaching-learning process used have an inhibiting or enhancing effect on future attitudes toward school and learning?

Over the last few years, much of the experimentation with newer ways of teaching mathematics and arithmetic in both the elementary and secondary schools has given attention to affective outcomes. Reorganization of material and emphasis on discovery methods are designed to keep alive the excitement of mathematical thinking and retain positive emotional reactions, as well as to improve understanding and skills in mathematics.

Active outcomes. When we speak of the active dimension, we are thinking first of overt motor activity and skills in doing things, the carrying on of actual observable or productive behavior—writing, computing arithmetic problems, building a house, making a cake, driving a car, painting, speaking a language—the *actual* doing of anything.

Our problem becomes complicated here because we want two levels of action as outcomes of teaching and we need to distinguish between the two. First we may want to develop the skill itself as in typing or speaking a foreign language. Second, we may want to use the act as evidence of cognitive and affective learning.

When a student gives an appropriate response to a test item, he has demonstrated only the skill of producing a particular bit of verbal behavior under a particular stimulus situation. The teacher may infer that this indicates certain understandings and feelings, but the only thing he can be certain about is the actual verbal behavior. To say or write, "Christopher Columbus discovered America in 1492," is an action response. To recite a poem that has been learned "by heart" is an action response, as is quoting rules of grammar or solving a quadratic equation. These activities may or may not indicate understandings or appreciations. Failure to distinguish these two levels in identifying expected outcomes accounts for much ineffective teaching.

Traditional foreign language teaching defined its outcomes as belonging primarily in the cognitive range. Students were first supposed to understand vocabulary, grammatical structure, and relationships with their native language and only eventually were they to develop some skill in reading, writing, and speaking the foreign language. Recently, a great deal of instruction in foreign language has turned the expectation around and defined its outcomes as belonging primarily in the active range. Students are taught more directly by the aural-oral approach—to listen, hear, and speak and to attach what they hear and say to objects, activities, and events—to develop the skill first and then expand to the other outcomes. Many experts claim that, in the long run, cognitive and affective outcomes in foreign language are noticeably improved by the initial focus on active outcomes.

It is difficult to find immediate, direct, or active outcomes of any great importance in teaching that Christopher Columbus discovered America in 1492. As evidence of cognitive and affective learning, speaking skills, writing skills, or test-taking skills may be enhanced. In a project activity, the manual skills involved—for example, in making models of the Nina, Pinta, and Santa Maria—may be important in themselves as well as being pathways to and demonstrations of cognitive and affective learnings. Skill improvements in reading, writing, listening, observing, studying, and interacting with others may be enhanced by this topic as by any other.

But the real pay-off in the active mode in relation to the topics of history is presumed to come much later in the temporal life of the individual. In the long run, in the rationale of American schools, the Columbus-discovery concept is part of a cumulative long-range development of cognitive and affective learnings, which is intended to result in certain kinds of citizenship activities and civic participations in the after-school years. The overt behavior of adults as participators in government, as voters, public officials, and makers of public opinion is the eventual target of such study. Whether or not such outcomes actually occur depends partly upon the teacher's awareness of such relationships while planning and carrying out instruction.

The above discussion is not intended to denigrate philosophies of education that place less emphasis upon the active domain. Some students will be impelled to engage in adult activities of scholarly study of history or avocational reading of history as a result of the accumulation of learnings in this area. These, too, are a form of active behavior. When the teacher looks at the active domain he must ask himself what *activities* are implied or desired in the instructional process and what their anticipated results are for the future behavior of the learner.

THE TEACHER ANALYZES THE LEARNERS

Having some idea of the expected outcomes, the hoped for changes in learners as a result of the prospective teaching activities, the teacher must also have some idea of the present characteristics of the learners he is working with.

He may start with a very undifferentiated picture of thirty or forty young people who are "about average" and "don't know very much." Even here he has some concept of "average" and certain assumptions of what they do know. At the other extreme, the teacher might have a voluminous case history of each child and have these well assimilated with data on interrelationships and group structure, so that his knowledge of the class is extremely detailed. Somewhere between these two extremes is the typical teacher and class.

Much time and energy is wasted in classrooms by teachers who do not know students well enough to specify their present status before attempting to change or improve it. Since the learner can only move toward expected outcomes from where he is *now*, productive teaching must start from his present status in order to help him change. If we assume too low a status, time will be wasted in repetition of information the children already know, in activities they can already perform, or in trying to develop attitudes that already exist. If we assume too high a status, children will be unable to perform as expected.

What does the teacher do in analyzing a class?

1. Uses a general knowledge about the characteristics of children of a particular age group.
2. Uses existing concepts about average behavior and its range.
3. Observes and listens to children in order to compare and contrast them to these concepts.
4. Uses school records and test data to assess their status.
5. Notes individual differences among children, especially those that may be helpful or harmful to the projected learning activities.
6. Engages in specific assessment procedures such as pretests, achievement tests, directed discussions, interest inventories, teacher-pupil planning, preliminary assignments, or the gathering of special data on individual students.

17

Both the teacher who says "this class can't learn because they have low IQ's," and the one who says "Mary has difficulty in reading, needs help in vocabulary development, but does very well in arithmetic," have made an analysis of the learners, although at very different levels of competence.

THE TEACHER SPECIFIES THE OBJECTIVES TO LEARNERS

With some idea of where the class is and where he wants to take them, the teacher is in a position to make specific decisions about what will constitute change in the right direction. If one of our expected outcomes in a high school English class is greater appreciation of poetry, and if we know that the class or particular individuals in the class dislike poetry, what specific changes will we work for and how far will we expect to get over a particular period of time? What specific changes will we expect to see at the end of the school year? If we want Johnny to read better, what is wrong with his reading now and what specifically do we want to change in his reading habits or skills? How can we find out if these changes take place?

The more appropriate and specific we can make these immediate objectives, the more productive our teaching is likely to be.

With a fairly clear picture of the specific changes to be wrought, our teacher is now in a position to select the specific subject matter to be dealt with and the most appropriate materials to be used. Parallel with these selections, the teacher also makes decisions about the methods to be used in bringing together the class and the material.

It is here that the teacher's knowledge of the field, of available text and supplementary materials, of technological aids, and of various methods of dealing with students becomes crucial to the teaching process. The teacher must decide what information is appropriate, how it should be organized, and what materials are most useful in presenting it. He must also select the most appropriate ways of presenting the material. For example, should he present the information orally, by assigned readings, through demonstrations, with audio-visual techniques, or by the use of programmed materials or teaching machines? Should he use student projects, and if so, long-range or short-range projects? Should he rely heavily upon outside assignments or concentrate upon work in the classroom as a laboratory setting? How should he balance the various methods?

Many of these decisions are actually made on the basis of tradition or school regulations. The institution may prescribe a textbook for the entire class or may discourage the provision of a variety of materials. In some teaching situations, practical problems may limit the choices of the individual teachers; in other situations, teachers may have wide latitude in making such decisions.

So far in this discussion, the students have not been involved except as they provided data for the teachers decisions. The teacher now involves the students in planned activities, which should result in the students' progressing toward the planned outcomes. The teacher creates learning situations that will stimulate students to listen, read, write, discuss, ask questions, perform tasks, solve problems, fabricate objects, think critically, or engage in other activities appropriate to the expected learning.

Since learning depends upon what the learner does, activating the class becomes crucial in achieving the objective.

It is in this segment of the analysis that the teacher uses the methods and materials he has planned to direct and guide the continuing activities of the students. By telling, explaining, demonstrating, assigning, encouraging, reprimanding, and giving instructions, he exerts verbal control over the activities of the class. By listening, observing, and evaluating production, he assesses the progress of the students. By making suggestions, redirecting efforts, and introducing new materials and activities, he gives continuous guidance to the learning activities.

It is apparent that there are tremendous variations in the skills of individual teachers in performing the functions of involving and directing students and their activities. Most of us have certain strengths, which we exploit in directing the learning process. Few of us completely achieve the skill of doing the right thing at the right time to achieve the best possible enhancement of learning. Some writers speak of the "teachable moment," implying that the learning process is enhanced if the teacher performs a particular teaching act when the conditions of the learning situation are ripe for it. Perhaps, effective teaching might be analyzed in terms of the frequency with which the teachable moment is adequately utilized.

THE TEACHER PROVIDES SITUATIONS
FOR USING THE LEARNINGS INVOLVED

It is commonly thought that learning is made effective or has long-range value if the learner has the opportunity to use his new concepts, attitudes, and skills in situations beyond those in which they were learned. Thus, the teacher provides opportunities for practice, for use, or for trying out learnings in new contexts. He may provide such opportunities by incorporating the use of previously learned material in plans for the next learning situation, by encouraging its use in situations that have reality to the students, or more conventionally, by providing limited practice opportunities.

THE TEACHER EVALUATES THE OUTCOMES
OF THE PROCESS

19

Obviously, some continuous evaluation of progress has been going on throughout the teaching-learning experience, even if only on a very informal level. Here, we are concerned with an attempt to find out if the desired or predicted outcomes have actually occurred. Does the student have more adequate concepts, information, or knowledge? Doess he think differently? To what extent does he feel differently in relation to the area under consideration? What can he do now that he could not do before? Such an evaluation is not as easy as it might seem.

In actuality, most formal evaluation in American schools tends to check only the verbal behavior of students. Typical are pencil and paper tests, in which students create verbal responses or indicate their recognition of written materials. From these responses, the other behaviors are inferred, not measured directly. If the teacher desires the student to *understand* some aspect of the operation of the federal government, this understanding or lack of it cannot be examined directly. It can only be inferred by the teacher from what the student says, does, or writes. This is true of most cognitive and affective outcomes at the most simple levels. Active outcomes are easiest to evaluate directly. The skill of typing at a certain speed and with a certain level of accuracy can be checked by direct performance. The skills of baking a cake or driving a car under given conditions can be checked directly. A student can demonstrate that he can verbalize a given quotation.

Most teachers evaluate less formally and less systematically by impressionistic assessment of student behavior. They use available evidence to infer changes that have occurred. For example, changes in the level of class discussion are taken to indicate changes in interest and understanding. Increased interest in literature is deduced from data on increased use of the library. Participation in student government is assumed to indicate some level of citizenship behavior.

If the teacher has been able to specify the objectives of teaching in behavioral terms in his initial planning, he is more likely to be able to evaluate the actual outcomes.

THE TEACHER AS A PERSON IN THE INSTRUCTIONAL PROCESS

The above analysis may seem to indicate that teaching is a highly rational process in which the teacher follows the logic of the instructional process and obtains predictable results. If this were true, there would be less variation in teaching. Returning to the concept of teaching as art and to Mark Hopkins and a student on a log, teaching is a highly individualized process in which the teacher's personality, in interaction with students, is a highly personal variable. Two teachers dealing with the same material and having very similar objectives will present very different pictures to the classroom observer. Different teachers will serve as significant models for different children.

There is considerable evidence that the particular personality characteristics of the teacher have a discernible influence on the behavior, learning, and adjustment of pupils (1; 7, pp. 506-82; 11; 12). However, there is little evidence, except in extreme cases, that certain personality characteristics are more desirable than others for teaching in general. Studies have not been able to demonstrate consistently that, for example, a well adjusted person makes a better teacher than one with definable maladjustments. Increasingly, it is being accepted that effective teaching depends upon appropriate matching of a particular personality with a particular teaching situation. It is quite possible for a teacher to do an outstanding job in one situation and a very poor job in another.

Teachers are individuals who have their own life styles and needs, and the pupils they work with have theirs. It is fortunate when the interaction of these two sets of factors can mesh to the enhancement of both. Seldom can this be completely true for a teacher and an entire class.

A complete treatment of personality analysis as applied to teachers is not possible in this brief discussion. To illustrate the type of thinking that is being done on this topic, let us look at only one dimension of personality and follow its implications. Several studies have attempted to isolate a personality variable that has been referred to as "tolerance of ambiguity." People who have a high tolerance level tend to be comfortable in unstructured situations, to be willing to let things develop, to have little need to exert close control over situations or other people. In dealing with others, they are more likely to be permissive and flexible. At the other end of the scale, those who have a low tolerance level tend to be more comfortable when things have a clear-cut structure and are carefully organized and planned. They tend to be more directive and rigid. They prefer yes and no answers to maybes.

In working with pupils, a teacher of the first type is more likely to encourage creativity, critical thinking, varied activities, and long-range outcomes. A teacher of the second type is more likely to emphasize "right" answers, specific responses, set procedures, routine activities, and a controlled teaching situation. They will organize very different learning situations and expect rather different outcomes. Individual pupils may prefer one approach to another; some will flourish more under one approach, others under the other. Obviously, as in all personality descriptions, most of us fall between these two extremes and most pupils in a school lifetime will come in contact with a varied assortment of teachers as perceived along this dimension.

It is clear that one of these types is not necessarily preferable to the other, but that each represents a somewhat different instructional role and anticipates somewhat different results as outcomes of instructional activities.

THE AUTHORITY OF THE TEACHER

In instructing or controlling a class, what authority does a teacher have? It may be helpful to categorize the different kinds of authority that can exist in a classroom setting, and to analyze some of the implications of their use (9, 12, 13).

At least seven sources of authority can be identified:

1. Physical superiority.
2. Formal or institutional authority.
3. The love relationship.
4. Psychological wisdom.
5. The authority of superior knowledge.
6. Superiority in thinking processes.
7. Skill in the teaching processes.

These seven sources, in effect, become types or kinds of authority. The authority stemming from physical superiority is a very different kind of authority than that stemming from superior knowledge. Authority is exerted in the interaction of the teacher with students. At any one time, such interaction probably calls upon several kinds of authority in different proportions depending upon the teacher, the student, and the situation. Value judgments may be applied to the efficacy of particular kinds of authority in particular situations.

PHYSICAL SUPERIORITY

Physical superiority is illustrated in the statement, "I'm bigger than they are." Much discussion of corporal punishment seems to assume that this authority is either basic or extremely important. Historical descriptions of teaching indicate that the assertion of physical superiority has frequently been a primary mode of control. In early-nineteenth century country schools, the initial battles between schoolmaster and older pupils determined who would exert the authority. Hopefully, in modern schools this mode is reduced in importance. Yet, for some pupils and teachers, the fear and threat of the assertion of physical authority is perceived as a major avenue of control.

With the development of compulsory and almost universal education, a complex school system—girded by laws, regulations, customs, and institutional arrangements—has developed. The teacher and students are inheritors of and subject to this complex, which gives the teacher what might be called formal or institutional authority. In actual practice, this kind of authority is probably most widely depended upon as the major method of control and the structure for instruction. The expectations of the impersonal system set limits for both student and teacher, with formal sanctions for violation of these limits. The formalized customs of "marking," "homework," "class organization," "promotion," "schedules," "textbook selection," and customary teaching procedures constitute a large part of the actual authority of the teacher in typical school practice.

THE LOVE RELATIONSHIP

Coercion and seduction are two major forms of control. The first two forms of authority would belong under the first heading, the love relationship under the second.

The love relationship refers to the personal relationship between teacher and child that involves a positive, warm emotional contact and encourages the psychological process of identification. When the child perceives the teacher as a significant figure, he may identify with him, seek to emulate or imitate him, and follow his instructions because of the personal response. The teacher becomes a loving parent surrogate. This form of authority is particularly strong in the primary grades, properly becoming attenuated with increasing maturity on the part of the child. Yet, in senior high schools, there are some teachers who inspire devotion and emulation on a personal level.

PSYCHOLOGICAL WISDOM

More sophisticated than the love relationship, but akin to it, is the authority we have labelled psychological wisdom. The teacher with a depth of understanding of children—their developmental sequences, motivations, and problems of living—who has a working knowledge of how to deal with these factors, has a kind of authority of expertness with great power. Such wisdom can be used in a manipulative way or it can be used as a good counselor uses it, in helping children grow according to their own best potential.

This type of authority and the remaining three could be thought of as types of a more general authority, called "the authority of expertness."

THE AUTHORITY OF SUPERIOR KNOWLEDGE

When the teacher has strength in the role of "one who knows," the information and knowledge he has confers great authority. The person who is respected as an expert in his field, who can be sought out to get pertinent answers, comes to be respected by students as an authority.

As in all types of authority, violation of the characteristic of superior knowledge can result in a loss of authority. The teacher who does not know, who makes serious errors in the presentation of information, may easily lose respect and have great trouble regaining his authority in some other way. This is not to say that the teacher must know everything. One of the characteristics of the expert is his ability to freely admit his ignorance and his willingness to investigate to find the right answer.

SUPERIORITY IN THINKING PROCESSES

This willingness to find out leads to the sixth kind of authority, superiority in the processes of thinking. Somewhat distinct from knowledge or information is the ability to analyze, synthesize, perceive relationships, and organize a sequence of ideas. Whether the characteristic mode is careful and logical convergent thinking or more creative, open, and imaginative divergent thinking, the teacher's ability to solve problems— to think his way through a situation—tends to provide him with an additional kind of authority in his interactions with the students.

SKILL IN THE TEACHING PROCESSES

Although partially dependent upon some of the other modes of authority, expertness in the teaching processes may be one of the most significant authorities a teacher can possess. A frequent complaint of college students, often voiced as, "He knows his stuff, but he can't put it across," applies to the instructor with the authority of knowledge, but not the authority of teaching skill.

The complex processes described earlier in this chapter as a model of the teaching process require great skill. The teacher who masters these skills to a high degree will have all the authority he needs in the classroom. We are all aware of the contrast between the teacher who never has a discipline problem and the one who is constantly losing control of his class. Usually, the learning situation in such extremes parallels the discipline situation. Careful observation and analysis will usually reveal a wide difference in the teachers' mastery of teaching skills.

Mastery and application of the "authority of expertness" should make dependence upon institutional controls and primitive physical superiority less and less important. Contemporary theories of human behavior and learning as well as empirical investigations of classroom teaching and learning tend to confirm this analysis.

TEACHERS' INFLUENCES IN INSTRUCTIONAL ACTIVITIES

The term "authority" has been used in the preceding section in order to focus on the kinds of "power" the teacher has. The word "control" has been used in a common-sense way. In order to exert "control" of the learning process, the teacher must use his "authority" to influence the class.

It has been said that the only thing the teacher can "control" is his own behavior. In order to exert influence, he must control his own behavior in ways best calculated to affect others. His selection of stimulus materials, his decisions on teaching strategies, his method of presentation to the class, his verbal instructions, and his response to classroom events are all aspects of his own behavior that influence the behavior of others.

A number of investigators have studied the influence of teachers in various categories of their behavior. Among the most fruitful investigations are those that have studied verbal behavior in the classroom (7, pp. 247-328, 683-714; 9, pp. 187-217; 12, pp. 251-60).

VERBAL BEHAVIOR AS INFLUENCE

Flanders has indicated that in the average classroom, someone is talking two-thirds of the time. The range of frequency of talk obviously goes well above and below this estimate. It has further been estimated that, of the talk that goes on, two-thirds of it is done by the teacher. Thus, in many classrooms the teacher is talking 50 per cent of the time (approximately 44 per cent on the average). Thus, whatever the teacher's source or kind of authority, he exerts it or attempts to influence pupils largely through verbal behavior. Through his verbal behavior, he may encourage or inhibit the behavior of pupils, verbal or otherwise, varying the pattern of interaction in the classroom.

Flanders further categorizes classroom talk into teacher talk and student talk. Teacher talk may be classified as exerting direct or indirect influence. Types and amount of student talk can be seen as evidence of the kind of influence the teacher exerts.

Direct influence can be seen in such activities as lecturing and giving information, giving directions, and criticizing or justifying the authority of the teacher or institution. Indirect influences are those that encourage student involvement and participation, as in such verbal activities as praising and encouraging, accepting student ideas and feelings, and asking questions.

As the students respond to these influences, they may answer questions, initiate their own comments, engage in activities as directed, or use their own initiative in setting up appropriate or inappropriate learning activites. As the teacher controls his own behavior, he exerts influence to control the behavior of students.

Considerable evidence is accumulating concerning the differential effects of the teacher's direct and indirect influences on the students' resultant behavior. The implications should be evident as we look at learning processes in Parts Two and Three of this volume.

TEACHERS' NONVERBAL BEHAVIOR

Although verbalization forms a large part of classroom behavior, it implies the existence of other forms of behavior on the part of the teachers. Observing and listening are fundamental to the teacher's indirect influence on the students. Outside of the classroom, continued study, planning, creating and collecting teaching materials, and deciding about classroom activities are all aspects of the teacher's behavior that exert influence on his instruction. The teacher's physical behavior—for example, his gestures and mannerisms, which betray his attitudes—and the consistency of his behavior are all aspects of the influence he exerts. All behavior may be analyzed in various ways, some of which are more illuminating than others. Current research on teachers' behavior is expected to eventuate in methods of analysis that should be increasingly helpful to teachers.

THE SELF-MONITORING OF BEHAVIOR

It follows from the preceding discussion that rational control of one's own behavior (becoming a rational artist in teaching) is a desirable objective for teachers if they are to gain control of the teaching process. Clarification of one's characteristic sources of authority and the development of ways of exerting influence can be enhanced by increasing awareness of one's own behavior. As we learn to monitor our own behavior and bring it under greater control, our chances of increasing our effectiveness as teachers should be enhanced.

As Mark Hopkins was used as an introduction to the teacher as a person, so it will be necessary to look at the "log" as part of the teaching process. The existence of a particular physical setting and the use of equipment and materials of various kinds are as much a part of contemporary teaching as is the teacher himself. The particular setting, the materials and equipment available, the designated curriculum, community factors, and the nature of the instructional group may all be considered as tools available for the extension of the instructional process. In this sense, they serve as media for the exercise of the teacher's influence in much the same way as does the teacher's verbal behavior. Through appropriate use of the "log," the teacher's range of behavior is tremendously expanded. The teacher manipulates the environmental variables that he and his students "sit on" to create a learning situation. His understanding of their nature, availability, and use; his attitude toward them; and his skill in manipulating them govern a large part of the instructional process. It is the purpose of this chapter to help the teacher understand some of the uses of the environmental factors of the school, which are available to him for creating learning experiences for students.

ADDITIONAL ASPECTS OF THE TEACHING PROCESS

3

The physical environment of American schools varies tremendously, ranging from the remaining one-room schools with primitive equipment to school plants for thousands of pupils, costing many millions of dollars. Within these schools, not necessarily parallel with their cost or physical size, the provision of equipment and materials for use in the teaching process is equally varied. The availability of equipment does not necessarily imply that teachers are using it appropriately to extend their influence (9, pp. 253-67).

In our affluent society, within a wide range of differences, it is highly probable that the schools of a community will be consistent with the homes of a community in architecture, space, and equipment. The culture perpetuates itself by providing school buildings that influence teachers and students in the direction of the community norm. Consciously or unconsciously, the typical teacher uses the physical environment of the school to instruct the students in attitudes toward the protection and care of property and the importance of their physical environment. More subtle learnings, for example, in the use of color and harmony in decoration, and concerning values in interactions between people and things, are also transmitted.

Modern school plants tend to provide more opportunities for flexibility, variety, and functional use than did the more formal, more uniform classroom of an earlier era. This setting encourages particular kinds of behavior on the part of both teachers and students.

When John Dewey was organizing his experimental school in Chicago in the 1890's, he searched for appropriate furniture to supply the kind of environment he desired for an active, working class. A perceptive salesman is said to have told him that he was seeking equipment that encouraged *working*, while all conventional school furniture was designed to encourage *listening* (6, pp. 47-48). Today's schools have available a variety of furniture with both specialized and multipurpose use. The typical classroom today does not have "listening" seats fixed in permanent rows, but is flexible enough to lend itself to continuous rearrangement for various purposes. The imaginative teacher can reorganize classroom furniture and space for a variety of activities that encourage varied learnings.

27

THE CURRICULUM AS AN ENVIRONMENTAL VARIABLE

From the point of view of teaching and learning, the curriculum of a school may be thought of as all experiences provided by the school intended to influence the behavior of pupils immediately or in the future. Within the individual classroom, all of the activities of the teacher as described in the preceding chapter plus all of the behavior of pupils constitute the actual curriculum. More conventionally, we are likely to think of the curriculum in terms of the informational content, the general method or approach to instruction, and the specific learning activities.

The teacher's perception of the ground to be covered, his approach to it, and the learning activities he selects are fundamental aspects of the teaching process, referred to here as the curriculum in a classroom.

In contemporary American society in the modern world, the amount of existing knowledge is massive and is increasing at a rate that should be alarming to those responsible for its transmission. With or without awareness of this responsibility, the individual teacher makes daily decisions about what information to deal with and how to deal with it. The selection of any particular information or activity implies the rejection of some other phase of learning. On what bases do teachers select a particular curriculum?

Conceptions of the goals of human development and responsibility. Some teachers have a picture of a desirable outcome, of a type of maturity that individuals should achieve. Curriculum decisions are made on the basis of a hypothesis of how much various materials and activities will contribute to such a goal. Part Three of this volume makes explicit some of the ways of conceiving these goals and implies curriculum content and activities that are appropriate to them.

Conceptions of the learning process. Some teachers resolve the dilemma of increasing knowledge and the limitations of human learning by focussing on processes that give promise of helping the learner adapt to new situations, solve problems, and learn how to learn. Content and activities are selected on the basis of hypotheses about the potentials of the materials for impelling such processes. To such teachers, covering conventional materials is less important than stimulating students to deal with vital issues.

Many recent attempts at formal curriculum revision follow this principle. Discussions of the structure of knowledge or the structure of the disciplines emphasize ways to help the student "think like a mathematician," "like a scientist," or "like a historian." Materials designed to encourage the process of inquiry or the "act of discovery" are basing curriculum selection on the principle that content is valid as it encourages appropriate learning processes.

Minimum essentials. Some teachers have the notion that there are certain basic facts, skills, and attitudes that are minimally required of all people in our society. Their curriculum selection is based upon the mastery of such objectives.

Courses of study and syllabi. A teacher may perceive his behavior as controlled or limited by a published course of study or a syllabus provided by a recognized educational authority. Such documents have the force of external environment as they direct the teacher's behavior.

The more imaginative teacher uses such documents as "launching platforms," as points of departure for planning instructional activities. The more rigid or less secure teacher may be confined by them, limiting his objectives and procedures by the restricted perception presented by the documents.

It should be apparent that the teacher's beliefs and value system in regard to curricular selection are basic to the environment he provides in the classroom. The log on which he sits is partially constructed from these beliefs.

THE HIERARCHY OF MEANING

As teachers achieve deeper understanding of the learning process and construct their teaching processes to harmonize with it, a variety of experiences are planned for learners. As it becomes clear that learning depends upon what the learner does, provision is made for those materials and activities that encourage him to do the things required to achieve the expected outcomes of the teaching process. As the teacher increases his understanding of students and their particular stage of development, he can become sensitive to the kinds of situations that have significant meaning for them, situations that attract their attention and to which they react most fully. Each individual's perception of reality differs somewhat from another's; however, there is a hierarchy of educative situations that can be used in planning learning activities. In general, the more a situation involves the learner, the more impact it will have on learning.

The hierarchy presented here is an abstraction in which positions will shift for some learners or for certain learning situations. For example, tape recording is placed lower in the hierarchy than films. Yet, for language learning, participating in recording and listening to tape may mean more and be more direct than observing a film. If the desired learning outcome is an analytical grasp of a philosophical position, reading and discussing the works of a philosopher will have more meaning than baking a cake. If a student has reached the point of becoming concerned with the theory of relativity, reading Einstein may be more significant to him than observing the stars. The effectiveness for learning depends upon the particular learner and the particular objectives. Even so, for purposes of an analytical presentation, a hierarchical outline may be useful, conceived as both a temporal and a logical consideration for teaching.

29

IMMEDIATE EXPERIENCES

Dewey's analysis of education as the continuous reconstruction of experience implies the primacy of the everyday, unplanned experiences of the learner. "Show and tell" or the "sharing" period in the primary grades directly emphasizes this type of experience. Events that have actually happened or are happening are used as the basis for learning.

Learning to become (or becoming) an individual personality is dependent upon the direct experiences the infant and child undergoes as he grows and develops in a specific situation. The most fundamental kind of individual teaching takes place in psychological therapy where the client's current life experiences are reconstructed by the client and therapist together. Science instruction is begun when the child observes the physical world around him, perceives that it operates, and starts questioning how. In adolescence, social activities and the experience of relationships among people are the realities that have impact as immediate experiences.

To the extent that the teacher can be aware of the direct experiences learners are having, and can use them in planning instructional activities, teaching will be vital and applicable at a high level of meaning.

When the teacher plans or organizes a situation in which students are expected to act or react, the resulting experience may be considered contrived. The remainder of the hierarchy may be considered subclassifications of contrived experience.

The highest level of contrived experience is provided when the teacher approximates an immediate experience, when environmental variables are so manipulated that the student may have difficulty in perceiving the activity as nonnatural. Many social situations of interaction among students and teachers are of this nature. When happenings planned by the school are perceived and reacted to directly by the student, this level has been achieved.

The next level is perhaps best illustrated by naturalistic science experiments in which the student participates—in which he is encouraged to manipulate the equipment, observe results, and draw conclusions. This level provides a focus for experience that may, in some cases, be more conducive to specific learning than ordinary experience. This level may also be achieved in other areas of learning, as in the social studies where the political organization of the classroom is exploited for purposes of student government, or in English when the creative production of students is emphasized.

With older age groups, a parallel level is achieved when high school students produce and enact a play in preference to observing a play, a film, or a television production. At a slightly lower level, planned contact with reality enhances learning experience in activities such as field trips. Visits to the fire department, stores, courts, and other community institutions are contrived, but have a direct quality.

Limited Experiences. The significant characteristic of all of the preceding experiences is their multifaceted nature. They include opportunities for multisensory perception, feelings, complex thought processes, and active doing in the situation. They comprise the primary learning experiences from which all other experiences derive their meaning.

The majority of school experiences are more limited, less complex, perhaps more sharply focussed. In a descending order, these include realia and demonstrations, imaginative hypothetical situations, television, films, filmstrips and slides, and other visuals. Experiences derived primarily from the auditory environment are provided by tape recording, records, and radio listening.

Lowest on the scale of meaning are those experiences that depend on words, whether oral, written, or printed. Talk and writing refer to more comprehensive experiences. Printed matter such as textbooks, reference materials, pamphlets, periodicals, and the usual programmed learning material has instructional value to the extent that it draws upon and extends more primary experiences.

The teacher does not deal with isolated individuals, but with a group of people who are organized in a social structure (9). The interaction of pupils in a class is characterized by various patterns of friendship, enmity, cooperation, competition, acceptance, rejection, and role expectation. For various activities, the roles enacted by individuals will shift.

There are many ways for the teacher to utilize the social structure of the class to enhance or interfere with the teaching-learning process. The way in which classes are organized according to age and grade, ability and achievement, or other criteria will affect the conditions under which teaching occurs.

There are many other critical areas that influence the teaching process. The nature of the community, the experiences provided by mass media, and administrative arrangements in the school are among those with which the effective teacher must deal in planning instruction and creating a teaching environment. The effective teacher must somehow acquire a wide array of understandings concerning knowledge of purposes, materials, techniques, and appropriate attitudes toward learners and society, in addition to a mastery of skills in weaving these together in the complex process of teaching.

BIBLIOGRAPHY

1. BARR, A. S. et al., The Measurement and Prediction of Teacher Effectiveness. Madison, Wisc.: Dembar Educational Research Services, Inc., 1961. A monograph reviewing thirty years of research in teacher effectiveness. The lack of definitive conclusions may be surprising, but some of the material is fascinating.

2. BARUCH, DOROTHY W., New Ways in Discipline. New York: McGraw-Hill Book Company, 1949. An excellent statement of the point of view that by expressing our feelings we can gain control of our overt behavior. Beautifully written with many illuminating examples.

3. BLOOM, BENJAMIN S. et al., Taxonomy of Educational Objectives, Handbook I: The Cognitive Domain. New York: David McKay Co., Inc., 1956. KRATHWOHL, DAVID R. et al., Handbook II: The Affective Domain. New York: David McKay Co., Inc., 1964. Extremely useful attempts to classify the expected outcomes of education under cognitive, affective, and psychomotor domains. The third domain is not yet dealt with as fully as the first two.

4. COMMISSION ON TEACHER EDUCATION, Teacher Competence, Its Nature and Scope. Burlingame, Calif.: California Teachers Association, 1957. Reprinted 1961.

5. CRAM, DAVID, Explaining "Teaching Machines" and Programming. San Francisco: Fearon Publishers, Inc., 1961. An interesting description of programmed learning, in the form of a "scrambled text-book," illustrating the principles with which it is dealing.

6. DEWEY, JOHN, The School and Society. Chicago: University of Chicago Press, 1909.

7. GAGE, N. L., ed., Handbook of Research on Teaching. Chicago: Rand McNally & Co., 1963. Produced and copyrighted by the American Educational Research Association. A monumental and invaluable volume for anyone interested in the teacher and the teaching process. Of par-

ticular interest as reference for this section are articles by Stern, Getzels and Jackson, Medley and Mitzel, and Withall and Lewis.

8. LAMBERT, PHILIP, ed., *The Teacher and the Machine*. Madison, Wisc.: Dembar Educational Research Services, Inc., 1962. Recent studies of programmed learning are presented. One of many recent volumes in a rapidly growing body of literature on teaching machines, programming, and related topics.

9. NATIONAL SOCIETY FOR THE STUDY OF EDUCATION, *The Dynamics of Instructional Groups*, Fifty-ninth Yearbook, Part II. Chicago: University of Chicago Press, 1960. Focussing on the social structures of the classroom, considerable light is cast on the authority and influence of the teacher. See especially, pp. 30-50, 164-84, 187-224.

10. ———, *Social Forces Influencing American Education*, Sixtieth Yearbook, Part II. Chicago: University of Chicago Press, 1961.

11. RYANS, D. G., *Characteristics of Teachers*. Washington, D.C.: American Council on Education, 1960.

12. SILBERMAN, HARRY F., ed., "A Symposium on Current Research on Classroom Behavior of Teachers and its Implications for Teacher Education," *The Journal of Teacher Education*, XIV, No. 3 (1963). This entire issue is devoted to recent research on teacher behavior.

13. STILES, LINDLEY J., ed., *The Teacher's Role in American Society*. New York: Harper & Row Publishers, 1957.

14. WATSON, JOHN B., *Psychological Care of Infant and Child*. New York: W. W. Norton & Company, Inc., 1928. A short book, written for the layman. It seems curiously naïve and dated to the contemporary reader. An excellent example of premature psychological fashion.

PART TWO THE NATURE AND
CONDITIONS OF THE LEARNING PROCESS

To learn is to engage in an experience that affects the psychological functioning of the individual in ways that will result in changes in his behavior. The word "learning" is used to refer to both the process and the result. As a process, learning refers to the experiences the learner goes through, his internal and external activity, and his reactions to the situation in which he finds himself. As a product, learning refers to the changes that occur—the ways in which the learner is different or the actual change in his behavior. These changes may be temporary or relatively permanent.

We have already dealt with the outcomes of the teaching-learning process from the teacher's point of view. In this section, we will focus on what happens to the individual learner. What does he go through as he learns and what are the results?

EXPERIENCE

In any segment of space and time, the individual learner is embedded in a situation. In this situation, he responds to certain stimuli in particular ways. He acts and reacts to the situation. This interaction is what we call experiencing. The experience may be highly

WHAT IS LEARNING?

4

complex or relatively simple. It may involve the learner to a maximum degree and produce violent activity; it may be as simple as reading a book or as specific as making a check mark on a paper. At any rate, it involves the learner doing something under some condition of stimulation.

The term "doing" is used here in a very broad sense to include apparent inactivity as well as overt activity. Lying on the beach soaking up the sun is a kind of doing, as is day-dreaming. Analysis of the cognitive and affective domains of behavior has focussed attention on what the individual *does* when he thinks, when he enjoys, or when he values. The behavior of the learner may not be immediately visible to the outside observer; however, it is happening.

Experiencing is stressed here as a necessary condition of learning because there are other ways of changing behavior that are not properly called learning. We normally distinguish between maturation and learning, implying that in maturation, changes occur in the person and his behavior as a direct result of the process of growth and physiological change. It may be impossible to ascribe the changes to one process or the other, but the distinction has logical values.

Similarly, behavior may be changed directly by drugs, disease, surgery, brain damage, or accidental harm to the organism. A man whose leg has been amputated will have his walking behavior changed. This direct change cannot be called learning. However, as a result of this change, the man will be a changed individual in a changed situation and will undoubtedly engage in much learning experience as a result of the physical change. He will have to learn to adapt to the changes. This latter experiencing can be called learning.

THE LEARNING SITUATION

We are all continuously surrounded by myriad stimuli that are capable of affecting us. As I sit here writing, I am surrounded by the physical conditions of the room—books on bookshelves, filing cabinets, the desk and chair, a particular level of temperature, variations of light and shade. Outside the sun is shining brightly. I am aware of the noise of the oil burner shutting off. The tactile sensations of writing provide variations. I hear the dog barking outside and see cars slowing down on the street. Beyond these immediate physical stimuli, I am stimulated by my projection of future events—the contract deadline for a book, the planned activities of this evening and tomorrow. I glance at the clock and become aware that it is probably lunch time. I feel some sensation of hunger. A complete catalogue of my immediate situation could go on endlessly. There are also many potential stimuli that do not affect me at all.

In a sense, I select, or am affected by, certain aspects of the situation more than others. The significant stimulations affect me in such a way that I continue my writing activity. Shortly, the situation will change and I will do something else. That "something else" will, in some ways, be affected by the experiencing I have been doing.

Similarly, the student in the classroom is a complex organism existing in a complex situation. As a complex organism, his attention and activities are directed by his entire personality structure and long-range influences, as well as by the immediate classroom situation. To some degree, the immediate classroom situation will be different for each student in the room as his perceptions are directed by his own needs, motives, and previous learning. The stimuli that prove significant to Jack may have no affect on Bob.

For example, a high school social studies teacher is attempting to clarify the relationship between the executive and legislative branches of the federal government. He has outlined the structure of government and is now giving examples of the limitations of the President's power, especially with reference to Congress. This is important to him and he wishes it to be important to the class. He explains clearly and uses the chalkboard for diagrams and emphasis of key words. His immediate objectives are primarily cognitive in that he wants students to have a deeper understanding of how their government works. He also has affective objectives in that he wants students to feel the importance of government structures and appreciate the values of the checks and balances. The active domain is least important, except for the increase of verbal skills in talking and writing about this area.

Now let us look at the class members and see what they are experiencing. Bob's uncle is a congressman (too bad the teacher doesn't know this). He feels some personal identification with the process being described and is considering the system from the point of view of Congress. At the same time, he wonders how much relationship there is between the theory being expounded and the practical politics that are discussed in his home. He has been in Washington and has many recollections of the physical settings of the government. The teacher's words have many rich experiential meanings for him. Bob is thinking of going into politics and the material being presented is significant to him.

Elise is the daughter of Hungarian refugees. Her mother and father have just completed the naturalization process to become American citizens. There have been many discussions at home about the structure and function of the government as her parents have compared and contrasted this kind of information with their background experience. Elise sees it as most important to learn this material and in some ways it is fresher and newer to her than to Bob.

Jack has been absent with illness for three days and has missed some of the earlier presentations. He does not see how this fits in and he has already been somewhat overwhelmed in other classes by the necessity to catch up. Besides, his energy is still low as a result of the illness. His best reaction is to stop paying attention and move into daydreaming about more pleasant things. He has become psychologically absent.

Helen has a crush on the teacher. Anything he says is fine with her, but her acceptance is much more on the emotional than the intellectual level.

Joe sits in the back of the room and hears what the teacher says, but the diagrams on the board are fuzzy. Joe is nearsighted and nobody knows it. He does not know that other people see more than he does. He has never known any other way to see. Consequently, during much of his school career, visual presentations have been of minor significance. His record shows it.

We could continue around the class indicating the very different experiences of different individuals, from those whose out of school interests and problems overcome the classroom situation to those who accept the classroom situation on the basis of achieving satisfactory marks and grades with little concern for deeper meaning or highly significant learnings.

More learning is likely to take place if the learning situation is rich in potential stimulation. The more impelling the situation, the more likely is the learner to be affected by significant stimulation and to engage in reactions that permit change. A rich learning situation permits the learner to become involved in activities in which he can test new behavior or expand and deepen present behaviors. This involvement comes from a combination of the learner's immediate status and the appropriateness of the situation to that status. If the learner perceives the situation as significant to him, he will be impelled to react to it in ways that change him. He can then move on to the next situation as a changed person with a changed behavior potential. He may "know" more, understand better, perceive things differently, or think in a different way. He may feel differently about something, or his potential reactions may be more or less intense. He may be more or less ready to engage in new experiences. He may be able to perform with greater skill or to do something he could not do before.

Carried to an extreme, this interpretation would imply that the teacher has very little control over the learning situation. Each individual lives his own experiences in his own world with various degrees of overlapping of the worlds of others. The teacher and the objective situation he provides are simply one phase of that world and are subject to varied interpretations. The teacher can never know for sure what the learner is reacting to. Teaching becomes a matter of providing situations as rich as possible so that each individual may find appropriate nourishment for his own needs and appropriate opportunities for learnings that are significant to him.

However, an opposite interpretation can be drawn from this analysis. Recognizing the uniqueness of each individual's experience, it is still possible to restrict and concentrate his attention for a period of time so that the specific classroom task overcomes the other potential stimuli and the learner focuses on a rather narrow or intense segment of the situation. This view emphasizes the importance of control and the learning of quite specific things. In practice, it is obvious that both kinds of learning situations occur. The more creative open-ended kind of situation probably produces broader but less predictable learning products. These products derive their significance from the needs of the learner, and are perhaps more meaningful. The more restricted kind of situation probably produces learning products that are more specific, more controllable by the teacher, and more easily predictable.

STIMULUS, ORGANISM, AND RESPONSE

A common paradigm in considering learning uses three major sets of variables: external factors that can be considered stimuli, the S variables;

internal factors that are characteristic of the organism itself, the O variables; and the responses the organism gives to conditions of stimulation, the R variables. The discussion up to this point has emphasized the difficulty of separating these variables in any absolute way; however, for purposes of description, the distinction is useful.

Various learning theorists tend to be concerned with different variables. Some are more interested in the organism itself, others in the stimulating conditions, others in the responses of the learner. Some of the resulting theories will be described in the next chapter. For our purposes here, each set of variables will be considered separately.

THE S VARIABLES

Any stimulus or set of stimuli to which the organism is sensitive can become part of the learning situation. The sensorium of touch, taste, sight, hearing, smell, and kinaesthesia, in its complexities and interrelated patterns receives the primary stimuli from the world outside. Undoubtedly, there are features in the world to which we are not sensitive. Apparently, the bat has sensory equipment not directly available to man. The typical dog receives data from his sense of smell and range of hearing that are not available to the typical man. Individuals vary in their sensory acuity. It is possible that we are affected by stimuli of which we are unaware, as in some of the experimentation with subliminal stimulation. Some of the evidence about alleged extrasensory perception may indicate the presence of sensory modes that have not yet been analyzed or defined. In one way or another, the organism must be capable of receiving the signals that affect him.

The individual sees, hears, touches, and manipulates the objects in his environment in order to sense them. In general, multisensory stimulations provide more opportunity for learning than does stimulation by a single mode. Intensity of stimulation, however, may provide exceptions to this statement.

THE O VARIABLES

In any complex situation, the learner must interpret the stimuli, differentiate and combine them, and give them some meaning. We have already emphasized the existence of selective reception.

There is no simple or standard way of describing the complex organism that is the human learner. Let us arbitrarily select certain descriptive dimensions that will be useful for our purposes.

Perception. The organism is so constructed that his sensations are not discrete but are organized in patterns. The individual has learned from previous experience to perceive in certain ways. He has a tendency to organize sensations in a way that is characteristic of him. He gives a different level of significance to various sensations. He has learned to pick out certain aspects of a situation and to fail to note others.

Concept structure. Previous experience has similarly given the individual an organized picture of the world around him (correct or incorrect), which he uses to organize and categorize his perceptions, to fit them into their appropriate place. He gives meaning to the sensations in the sense that he relates them to things he already knows. In the process, both the sensations and the existing structure are likely to be altered.

Self-concept. As one fundamental phase of concept structure, the individual has a concept of who he is and how he fits into the world. The information coming from outside is screened in terms of its effect upon his view of himself. The person who sees himself as adequate and successful will respond to stimuli quite differently from one who anticipates failure.

Attitudes. The concepts the individual has are not purely intellectual or cognitive. They have a dimension of emotion or feeling. He has likes and dislikes, approvals and disapprovals, beliefs and disbeliefs. He is attracted toward some activities and ideas and tends to avoid others. These feelings develop into somewhat enduring attitudes that govern his "set" or response tendencies. A hierarchy of values develops, which may be called the attitude structure.

Needs. At the deepest levels of personality (and to some extent governing the preceding four dimensions), the organism has a survival and self-maintenance system that may be referred to as the needs structure. Some theorists define a need as a lack of something that, if present, would contribute to the continued survival of the organism or to a more harmonious operation of its behavior systems. More positively, other writers postulate a built-in growth potential that provides for the continued emergence of higher order needs as the sheer maintenance needs are satisfied. It is clear that in the physiologically developmental period of life, there is such a growth potential at least in terms of physical growth. Needs theorists contend that it is out of this basic biological tendency to survive and grow that the psychological needs develop. (This concept will be dealt with in greater detail in Chapters 7 and 13 of this volume.)

For our present purposes, it is sufficient to point out that the combination of satisfaction and frustration of needs provides a profound source of direction for behavior. There is considerable evidence that the predominant needs of an individual affect his perception, his way of conceptualizing, his value judgments, and his overt behavior. When a need exists and is unsatisfied, it becomes a major motive for learning, for modifying behavior so that satisfaction may be found.

Motives. When the individual senses an unfulfilled need, he seeks to do something about it. He is *moved* to do something. Motives may be of long or short duration. If I am in need of nourishment, I become aware of being hungry and am motivated to seek food. Having eaten, this motive is no longer effective. However, I have learned that this is a recurring need and that provision must be made for its satisfaction. I have an enduring motivation that causes me to seek enough money to be able to purchase food, to periodically stock the food supplies in the house, and to provide a whole armamentarium of such equipment as freezers, refrigerators, stoves, cooking utensils, and many other things, partly as assurance of continued satisfaction of this recurrent need. At the same time, needs for social status dictate the type and amount of such equipment with which I can live comfortably.

In a much more complex way a young man may have evaluated himself and his needs in such a way that he has decided it will be satisfying for him to become a doctor of medicine. Over many years, much of his activity is motivated by this decision and many temporary frustrations and discomforts are borne as he pursues the preparation for his profession.

Goals. The end product toward which we are motivated is a goal. The things and potential activities in a situation are ignored or acquire goal properties as the learner perceives them as worthy of being attended to and as useful for satisfying his needs.

Intelligence. There are many ways of defining intelligence. In this discussion, it will be most useful to think of intelligence as the ability to profit from experience. There are probably many factors in this ability and many degrees of it. Undoubtedly, some individuals are biologically superior to others in their potential to perceive and act appropriately in the world around them; and further differentiation occurs through the total influence of all of the dimensions previously described and the particular individual's opportunities and experience. At any given time, an individual's reaction to a learning situation will be affected by this ability to give meaning to the situation.

Skills. Related to intelligence, but usually thought of in relation to motor abilities and activity, the individual's skills in dealing with situations affect his perception and potential behavior. If he can perceive himself as engaging in effective activity, he will handle the situation in a way quite different from that which would be true if he were unskilled. The combination of the repertory of skills available and the skills required by the situation sets up quite varied possibilities for experiencing.

Previous learnings and recollections of past events. Finally, all of these dimensions are modified by the present status of the individual's life history. His recognition of similarities and differences between current and past situations helps to structure his present reactions.

Additional descriptive dimensions might be used, but the preceding ten will suffice to present a model of the organism in a learning situation. These characteristics are not discrete but interact with each other in a dynamic way. If we symbolize the organism as a sphere with these ten (and more) internal areas, a change in one area will necessitate some readjustment in the others. A change in attitudes may result in some change in concepts, self concept, needs, etc. We may picture the model this way:

In a learning situation, the learner's immediate organization impels him to perceive certain aspects as being more significant than others, and he reacts to these aspects of the situation and responds in some way. The response has certain consequences for him; it affects him in some way and produces some change in the structure. Perhaps, a need formerly unsatisfied is now satisfied and there is some shifting of the boundary lines or a different area assumes more importance. Perhaps, in reacting to the situation, a skill has been improved and a slight shift occurs in the individual's self-concept ("I can do something I couldn't do before"); a goal may be perceived that was not effective before. To some extent, the individual learner has changed and now moves on to a new situation with a different potential for response.

To bring the S variables and O variables together in a diagram, we can show the individual surrounded by a situation:

Some stimuli are received and accepted by the learner. Others are objectively present, but do not reach the learner. Some of the stimuli have greater importance to the learner, receive more attention, and exert more influence.

Finally, to introduce the R variables, we may complete the diagram with the outgoing arrows indicating the responses of the learner in this situation.

THE R VARIABLES

Learning depends upon what the learner does. It is his response to the situation that makes further change possible. Any actions or reactions to a situation constitute response variables or overt behavior. In considering teaching in Chapter 2, we dealt with the behavioral outcomes of learning. Looking now at the process of learning, the same classification will serve.

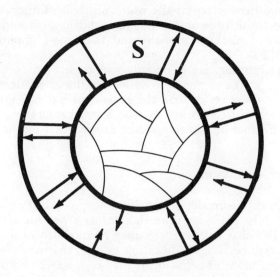

We are likely to think first of a response as overt observable behavior and, therefore, as belonging in the active or psychomotor domain. This is the easiest kind of response with which to deal, and most experimentation in learning has of necessity dealt with such responses. But from the viewpoint of the learner, his emotional reaction or his nonverbalized thinking behavior are certainly equally important. The cognitive, affective, and active domains are all included in possible responses.

Suppose I were to ask you to memorize Hamlet's soliloquy. Let us assume that you are willing to do so—that your O variables today are in a condition such that the task is an attractive and possible one. Assume further that a copy of the soliloquy is available to serve as one set of stimuli. What would you do? Different learners would approach the task in different ways. You might first read it silently (look at the page, make appropriate eye movements, move from line to line, think about its meaning—do all the things you long since learned to do in silent reading). You might read the whole passage aloud. You might ask someone else to read it to you (engage in listening activity). You might discuss its meaning with someone else. You might tape record yourself reading it aloud and then listen to the tape. You might feel pleasure or displeasure as you went through these activities. You might organize or analyze the passage in various ways. You might read it over and over and then close your eyes and try to visualize it. You might eventually try saying it aloud with the copy covered. If you did enough things right, you would eventually be able to quote it on demand. You would then be able to do something you could not do before.

To take any of the above possibilities of your behavior and completely catalogue all the things you did would be almost impossible. The minutest details of your response are all involved in the final learning outcome. Some people would attack this task as one of rote memory. They might learn little more than to repeat the words on signal. Others might engage in much more cognitive behavior and the total result would be different. Still others would react emotionally and their most important learning would reflect this.

In analyzing learning, we frequently concentrate on specific responses and tend to forget the tremendous variety of things the learner is doing. As a result, we often claim that the individual did not learn. It would probably be more correct to say that he learned something we were not watching for, because he was responding in ways that did not concern us.

THE INEVITABILITY OF LEARNING

It follows from the model of the learning process described here that learning must take place anytime the learner reacts in a situation that affects him. His behavior tendencies may be modified in many ways, but modified they will be. The modification may be the strengthening or fixation of a present mode of behavior. It may be a weakening of a tendency. It may be some completely new way of doing something. It may be an increment of skill in a performance or the reduction of a skill already acquired. It is not always possible to predict or assess the learning, but the logic of this description insists that some learning will take place.

The learning product may not be socially desirable. We learn to steal and lie just as we learn to act honestly or to tell the truth. We learn false information just as we learn correct information. Our behavior develops in accordance with our reactions to situations.

44

LEARNING AND THE CONSEQUENCES OF BEHAVIOR

This discussion has not yet made explicit the factors that tend to fix the change in behavior or to produce one outcome rather than another. These factors are implicit in the discussion of the individual variables. The consequences of one's responses provide the feedback that governs probable future behavior. Some theorists talk of this in terms of reinforcement, others in terms of rewards, others in terms of need or drive reduction. The common theme is the general idea that the individual receives information confirming the behavior as having consequences that are desirable to him.

Take the case of two college students who, after low grades on several tests, wish to do better and get advice on study habits. They both discover that, among other things, it is better to cut down on last minute cram sessions and to get a good night's sleep before the exam in order to come into the test session rested and ready to think. They learn this in the sense that, by following the new regimen, their grades on the next exam improve considerably. For one of the students, this consequence of her changed behavior is sufficient for her to continue following the new approach and change her pattern of studying. The other student, though the specific consequence was the same, slipped back into her previous pattern because she lived in a sorority in which staying up all night before an exam was "the thing to do," and the consequences of losing out in popularity and group conformity were too severe to take.

Hence, it is not only the specific consequence that fixes one's behavior, but the total consequences in terms of the individual's own motivational systems. We often learn to do things that are "bad for us" because we perceive them as being "good for us." We learn to do the things that are appropriate to our organismic structure and to avoid behaviors that do not give us satisfaction.

SUMMARY

The discussion here has presented a broad review of the learning process and has attempted to clarify what happens when one learns. It may be summed up in the following statements.

1. Learning is a process that involves behavior, sequences of events, and outcomes.
2. Learning results from experiencing. The learner must in some way act upon or react to a situation that impinges upon him.
3. Learning depends upon what the learner does. This involves how he perceives, how he thinks, how he feels, and how he acts. There can be no learning unless he responds in some way.
4. The end result of the learning process is some change in the learner, demonstrable by a change in his behavior, potential or actual.
5. The change in the learner tends to be fixed by the consequences of his behavior in terms of his own motivational systems.

Having taken a broad look at the learning
process, let us now turn to the sometimes
confusing aspect of varied descriptions of the
learning process and its details, which are
provided by various researchers and
learning theorists.

To date, there is no comprehensive theory
covering all aspects of learning. There is
considerable disagreement about the language
to be used in describing learning. Different
writers hold conflicting positions on the degree
of specificity or generality appropriate in
talking about learning. Some psychologists
become interested in certain kinds of learning.
Others have a particular theoretical set that
causes them to look at learning phenomena in a
particular way. Still others may have similar
views, but develop specific language patterns
or descriptive terminology in their theoretical
statements. Concepts of reward are not too
different from concepts of reinforcement, yet
there are subtle differences in the implications
of these two terms as they are used
in specific theories.

The layman is likely to think of a theory as
being true or false, right or wrong. Increasingly,
in the behavioral sciences, these concepts are
being replaced by such concepts as
adequacy of description and explanation,

LEARNING THEORIES:
THE SPECIFISTS

5

comprehensiveness of the theory in dealing with phenomena, and usefulness for prediction. In comparing two conflicting theories, we are likely to ask questions such as: How well does the application of this theory predict future events? How large a set of related phenomena does it deal with? How well does it describe and explain the phenomena under consideration?

Some theories are quite narrow in their scope, carefully limiting the phenomena they observe; such theories tend to be better for limited predictions. They usually involve interest in details and careful control of conditions.

Other theories tend to be very broad in scope, concerning themselves with broad principles and a larger conceptual framework. Still others are primarily descriptions of existing phenomena accompanied by attempts to conceptualize observations.

Learning theories range from quite specific concerns with particular stimuli and responses to explorations of the total personality of man in society and his resultant behavior systems, both overt and covert.

A further distinction may be made concerning the methodology of various theorists. Some tend to use carefully controlled, obejctively defind experimental situations to gather data and test their hypotheses. At the other extreme, some tend to use broadly based naturalistic observation and to deny the efficacy of careful control of the situation. Such methodology may or may not parallel the resultant outcomes of the theory.

In classifying and describing the main feature of selected theories, some violence will be done to details of the theories in a relatively brief overview. For convenience, the theories have been classified in three categories: the specifists, the field theorists, and the personality theorists. The latter two terms are commonly used in describing psychological theories. The term "specifist" is less common; it is selected here to indicate that these theorists are identifiable by their concern with very specific units of behavior. Their search tends to concentrate on specific stimuli and specific responses and to assume that broader aspects of behavior are summations of these. Their focus is on the specifics of the S and R portions of our model.

The field theorists are seen as concerned with perception, cognition, and action in a broader context. For them, a generally defined organism responds with more varied alternatives to a broader range of stimuli.

The central concern of the personality theorists is behavior as an accompaniment of the quality of being. Their focus tends to be on the individual organism more than on impersonal conditions of stimulus and response.

STIMULUS AND RESPONSE: the Specifists

An early stated and continuing theme in American psychology has been the analysis of very specific behavior and the general assumption that complex behavior is an adding together, a summation, of simple behaviors. Those psychologists who are intrigued with this theme tend to be concerned with describing peripheral activities in terms of observable stimuli and observable responses; they are much less concerned with the internal or central processes of the organism. This position has been maintained partly because of its historical roots in the development of psychology.

EDWARD L. THORNDIKE

As early as 1898, Thorndike published a theory of learning, based primarily upon animal experiments and using a trial-and-error model. Throughout the years, he expanded and developed this approach and did a tremendous amount of empirical work on its application to school situations (11, 22, 28, 29, 30, 31, 32). The unit of behavior was a relationship (an association or connection) between sense impressions and impulses to action. Faced with a situation, the learner will engage in a number of responses eventuating in the one that "solves" the problem. In repetitions of the situation, the incorrect responses will diminish and the correct response will become fixed. An illustrative experiment is that of a cat in a box with a rather complex release mechanism. The cat is hungry (or more properly, food deprived) and there is food outside. The cat's first activity is apparently quite random and varied. It takes considerable time before the cat responds in a way that unfastens the latch and permits the cat to get to the food. In continued trials, the time in the box is reduced as the cat makes fewer false moves and as the release behavior becomes more dependable.

It is notable that Thorndike does not postulate any "thinking" or ideational activity on the part of the cat. He is not concerned about problems of perception or interpretation of the situation. He postulates only two central processes, some sort of internal connection between sensation and response and the automatic effect of reward (food, hunger reduction) and punishment (lack of food, hunger discomfort) in stamping in and stamping out particular connections. Neither the precise nature of the connection nor the internal operation of reward seemed to be of great importance to Thorndike. The connection was talked about as if it were a direct bond of neurones across synapses in the central nervous system and as if the pairing of the action of that bond with a satisfying state of affairs in the organism somehow strengthened the connection. Though he expressed some general hypotheses about how this effect took place, the important thing in the theory was that *some sort* of connection took place and that the theorist was more interested in the external conditions and results than in the central process.

As applied to human learning, Thorndike's work stressed the specific responses of persons. It stressed the importance of motivation as a system of external arrangements of rewards and punishments. In analysis of school practice, it emphasized the necessity of causing children to learn the specific behavior they would need, and it reduced the stress on the processes of generalized transfer of learning. In practice, his theory seemed consistent with drill and habit formation and less applicable to learning based upon insight, understanding, and meaning.

Though described here as a "specifist" and important in the trend toward looking at behavior as a specific, Thorndike actually dealt in rather large units of behavior. There was little analysis of the specific sensory stimulus or the specific muscle response. The behavior he observed and the laws of learning he promulgated were quite broad and general.

IVAN PAVLOV

A Russian physiologist's experimental work with the conditioned reflex had considerable impact on learning theory in this country. Unlike Thorndike's rather broad definition of a unit of behavior, Pavlov's typical experimental concern was with a very narrowly defined unit of behavior, the reflex (11, 32). The prototype of his experimental work has entered the folklore and needs only a brief description here.

Under carefully controlled laboratory conditions, a harnessed dog was prepared by minor surgery so that the output of a salivary gland could be collected and measured. Meat powder was presented to the dog. Salivation occurred and the amount was measured. This was normally to be expected and it normally occurred. The dog was also tested with a bell or buzzer or other stimuli. Behavior appropriate to this stimulation occurred, but not salivation. Then the meat and the sound of the bell were presented, in some cases simultaneously, in others with the bell sound starting prior to the presentation of meat. Over a period of time, salivation occurred to the sound of the bell with or without the presence of meat. The meat and salivation to it are designated as the unconditioned stimulus and reflex, the bell and salivation to it as the conditioned stimulus and reflex. The dog had learned to salivate to the sound of the bell. His salivation had been conditioned. However, it was found that, in the long run, the conditioned reflex would deteriorate as shown by first decrease and then cessation of saliva flow unless it were occasionally reinforced by the unconditioned stimulus (meat).

Note that the dog had not learned to give a new response. He had learned to attach an existing response to a new stimulus. In Pavlov's interpretation and others consistent with it, there is again no mediation by ideas or meaning. This is an automatic pairing of stimuli so that either set can elicit the response.

Pavlov and his fellow workers also found that secondary conditioning could be done in the same way. For example, after the dog had learned to salivate to a bell, the pairing of a light with the bell would eventually produce salivation to the light. Theoretically, it seemed that such a substituting of one set of stimuli for another could build behavioral reactions far removed from the original stimulus.

JOHN B. WATSON

When Pavlov's work was introduced into the United States it found a field prepared to receive it. Watson, the founder of the behaviorist school of psychology, had announced his basic position in 1913; he depended heavily upon animal psychology as a basic provider of principles applicable to human behavior (37, 38). In his search for completely objective explanations of human behavior and for objective tools for research, Watson found the conditioned reflex an extremely useful model. He expanded the concept beyond the specific reflex to include responses that are more complex and nonreflexive in character. The unit of stimulus and response became the basic building block of behavior.

Watson himself did not build a systematic theory of learning as such, except insofar as his basic concern with the development of behavior is a problem in learning. To Watson, practically all behavior is learned. It is built by the pairing of stimuli and responses from earliest infancy. Conditioning provides the model for explaining this process. Given the original constitutional reaction potential of the infant, he is conditioned to respond in particular ways to particular stimuli. By building conditioning on conditioning over the years, the whole complex repertory of behavior is built up. Watson attempted to explain learning without using the concept of reward or reinforcement by maintaining that the response most frequently or most recently associated with a stimulus will be elicited by that stimulus.

EDWIN R. GUTHRIE

Following Watson in both time and approach, Guthrie developed his basic principles of learning in the 1930's (7, 11, 22, 32). Seeing Pavlovian conditioning as a special case in learning, consistent with but not the prototype of basic learning theory, he took a position that is extremely simple, but profound in its implications.

Guthrie is concerned with movements of the organism. For him, all behavior can be reduced to a series or complex of movements. Basically, learning to produce particular movements in connection with particular stimuli is "one-trial learning." The movements going on at the time that a particular set of stimuli are operating will be repeated the next time the same set of stimuli operates. What we have done under a set of conditions, we will continue to do under the same set of conditions. There is no need to postulate purpose, thinking, meaning, or reward. Reward or reinforcement seems to be effective only because it changes the situation. The behavior in the original situation remains unchanged not because it was rewarded, but because it last occurred under those stimulus conditions. We learn what we do.

The theory of "one-trial learning" is hard to accept because we all know how difficult it is to learn some things and how much repetition is sometimes necessary. Guthrie's system answers this objection very neatly with the proposal that in action any behavior is a very complicated series or mosaic of movements. Actual performance is made up of a myriad of movements, some of which will be incompatible with each other in the initial stages of performance. Putting together a complex activity is a matter of learning to inhibit some movements, fix others, and have one appropriate movement serve as a stimulus cue for the next. Furthermore, the exact same stimulus situation is seldom repeated precisely and totally. Thus, there are tremendous variations in actual performance even though the basic units of movement associated with stimuli are highly stereotyped.

The typical demonstration of Guthrie's position is provided by a cat in a particular kind of puzzle box (22). Contrasted to Thorndike's puzzle box, the release mechanism is extremely simple, consisting of a pole in the center of a glass cage. Any displacement of the pole will open the door.

A camera set to snap automatically with the opening of the door reveals the cat's position and movement at the time of release. The cat is introduced into the box from the rear and is allowed preliminary trials through the open door. Then, with the door closed, the movement of the cat is observed as he enters the box, touches the pole, and is released. The series of pictures of any one cat show a remarkable degree of stereotyping as he goes through a similar movement sequence each time to touch the pole, open the door, and leave. One cat might consistently back into the pole, another might touch it with the right shoulder, others would respond in other ways. The cat tends to perform the movements he had previously performed in the same situation, even if they are nonfunctional from the observer's point of view.

Since one movement becomes the stimulus for the next, variations in performance are explained as variations in the necessary movements as the cat enters the puzzle box. It is not necessary to postulate any reward or reinforcement even though food was available outside the box. The movement sequence is preserved not because it is rewarded but because the situation has ceased and the last performance has become the learned one.

As an explanation of the part of our behavior that is habitual and stereotyped, this description of the learning process may be useful. For more complex learning, or for what appears to be production of novel behavior, it is less convincing. In a sense, it explains the fixation of habitual activities, but it does not concern itself with the origin of the activities. Why does the cat move in the first place? How does he stumble upon the particular behavior that gets fixed? It seems to many critics that Guthrie's position ignores many of the basic questions about learning and directs itself to a very minor aspect of learning.

51

CLARK L. HULL

Where Guthrie's approach is apparently simple and casual, Hull's theories are extremely complex, detailed, and formal (11, 13, 22, 32). He prefers a mathematical language, using symbols that he has created and defined according to a deductive logic. He is concerned about precision of statements involving details of stimulus and response interaction. Consequently, it is difficult to give a broad statement of his position without doing violence to his work. Yet, his work has been so influential among learning theorists that its major features must be described.

For Hull, analysis of learning starts with several basic assumptions about the organism. First, given at birth are certain connections between receptors and effectors that provide the potential for particular stimuli to elicit particular responses. These stimulus-response units are by no means simple; they exist in myriad interconnections and interrelationships. The major problem of learning is the one that Guthrie ignores—how do some responses get established and others extinguished? Hull postulates basic needs in the organism as the motivation through which reinforcement of responses will occur. The need sets up a *drive* to activity. The *responses* that satisfy the need reduce the drive. This *drive reduction* provides the *reinforcement*, which makes it likely that the organism under similar conditions of stimulus patterns and drive will respond similarly. For example, the food-deprived rat in the maze has a need for nourishment. He will be driven to food-seeking activity. He will respond to those stimuli that are associated with food getting (either through natural or previously learned connections). The eating behavior in the presence of food reduces the need and the food-getting drive. The responses that led to this reinforcement tend to be retained; those that failed to do so will be extinguished.

So far, this seems relatively straightforward, but we have not yet reached the problems in learning that interest Hull. Given the above broad outline of how learning occurs, the details of relationship among stimuli, needs, and responses are critical. Are there time relationships in the receptor-effector sequence and in the reinforcement process that determine the establishment of particular responses? What establishes the strength of one habitual behavior as compared to another? How are connections among the impulses retained in the nervous system? Does the intensity of a stimulus influence the response? Is there a hierarchy of behavior patterns? If so, what determines them?

Questions like these, and his particular mode of answering them, make Hull's position unusual and rigorous. He does not answer in terms of gross observable behavior as does Guthrie. Neither does he answer in terms of actual neurophysiological structure, nor in literary, descriptive analyses. He answers in terms of postulates about afferent and efferent neural impulses, from which derive theorems about stimuli, drives, responses, and habit strength. The predictions rising from these theorems can, to some extent, be checked experimentally.

Learning, for Hull, is to be understood as a matter of associating stimuli and responses under conditions of drive, leading to reinforcement through need reduction. How learning takes place is to be answered by quite specific analyses of the relationship of neural impulses set up by quite specific stimuli acting upon equally specific response potentials.

B. F. SKINNER

Skinner's point of view has recently received increased attention as a result of the current interest in teaching machines and programmed learning (11, 12, 25, 32). It provides the theoretical basis for much of the work that has been done with the programmed learning principle.

Starting with the intention of describing learning and behavior from the observer's point of view, Skinner has avoided the intervening variables and speculations about neural activities that are characteristic of Hull. Instead, he has described in detail the external conditions in which certain kinds of learning take place and the behavior of the organism under these conditions. Doing his basic work with rats and pigeons, his description has perhaps carried more implications for human learning than the work of the other specifists.

Most S-R theorists have assumed the existence of a stimulus, which sets off a response. If no external stimulus was apparent, it was assumed that the unobserved internal environment provided such stimulation. By the very task he set himself, Skinner cannot permit this assumption and must observe a number of responses with no known stimuli. He, therefore, defines two kinds of response—the usual response "elicited" by known stimuli and the "emitted" response, which occurs without known stimuli. The first type is known as "respondent" behavior, the second type as "operant" behavior.

Respondent behavior is learned according to the classical Pavlovian model. Since it is concerned with stimuli, it is known as S-type conditioning.

More important to Skinner is operant behavior, which is concerned more with responses than with stimuli. This is known as R-type conditioning. The problem of training animals or teaching humans is to fix the appropriate responses. The organism is capable of many responses, and the problem of the experimenter is to cause the appropriate ones to be maintained. In doing this, Skinner has essentially changed the usual S-R formula into an R-S formula.

In other words, when a desired response is emitted, a reinforcing stimulus is presented. This tends to condition the response. It is the reinforcement following the response that is important. For example, a food-deprived rat may be trained to press a lever by presenting him with a food pellet when he presses the lever as desired. Even a rather complex series of responses can be developed in this way, such as training the animal to press a series of levers in a particular sequence or training a pigeon to peck at a food delivery disc when a light is on but not when it is off. Similarly, failure to reinforce will result in the extinction of a response.

In uncontrolled situations, we are similarly conditioned by the occurrence of a particular response followed by a reinforcement. Apparently, for Skinner, most behavior can be described in this way.

Skinner shows little concern about a theory of motivation or attempts to infer internal processes. The reinforcement of conditions seems to be taken for granted in a common-sense way. Food is reinforcing to a rat or a pigeon. Knowledge of correctness is reinforcing to a learner in school. The conditions that result in conditioning are reinforcing. The actual data dealt with is the observed behavior of the organism under observed conditions.

One of the consequences of this external approach has been careful analyses of some of the experimental arrangements under which conditioning takes place. One important factor so studied has been schedules of reinforcement.

If a pigeon must peck a disc ten times before receiving food, but does receive the food at every tenth peck, he will respond with continued pecking at a fairly high rate. If, on the other hand, he is reinforced with food at regular time intervals, provided he does a minimum of pecking, his pecking will become minimum, speeding up somewhat as the appropriate time draws near. The first set of conditions is known as fixed-ratio reinforcement, the second as fixed-interval reinforcement. Similar training arrangements apparently work with other species as well and may give some hints about controlling human behavior in learning situations.

Similarly, partial reinforcement has been compared with 100 per cent reinforcement with regard to maintenance and extinction of responses. If a pigeon was trained in a situation where each appropriate response resulted in food, he quickly learned the response. However, if reinforcements stopped, the response soon stopped also. On the other hand, when the pigeon was trained with variable reinforcement, so that a response was reinforced from time to time, but not every time, the response was remarkably resistant to extinction.

This kind of analysis of situational variables that affect learning obviously carries some interesting implications for classroom teaching. It is precisely these implications that have undergirded the development of teaching machines and programmed learning. The Skinner type of program breaks information to be learned into small sequential units or "frames." To each of these the learner makes a response. Ideally, if the material is organized properly, he will make the correct response and will be *immediately* informed of its correctness. Hence, there is immediate positive reinforcement, tending to fix that response and permit movement to the next frame. The learner is permitted to move at his own rate and get appropriate reinforcement without having to wait for the whole class and receive the nonsystematic reinforcement, which is all a teacher can give in a group situation.

There are other types of programmed material, based on other theoretical approaches; however, this is one of the few major current ideas in teaching that is directly related to a theory of learning.

SUMMARY OF SPECIFIST THEORIES

These theories have been presented briefly, partly to provide a historical perspective on one aspect of learning theory. Psychologists who are inheritors of the specifist tradition tend to look for specific stimuli and observable responses. The O variables are less important to them than the S and R variables, and they are more concerned with overt observable behavior than with speculation about the broad dimensions of individual motivation. Methodologically, they tend toward the objective, carefully controlled experiment with the careful specification of variables.

On the other hand, modern inheritors of the tradition are becoming increasingly concerned with problems of cognition, the organization of behavior, and the processes that mediate (or come between) the stimulus and the response. These interests should eventually provide a bridge between the tradition described here and the one described in the next chapter.

Readers who are familiar with psychological literature may attempt to equate the theories described as "specifist" with "behaviorism." There is some relationship, but there are theorists who classify themselves as behaviorists in methodology who concern themselves with areas that could not be classified as specifist. Conversely, Thorndike, for example, clearly belonged to the specifist tradition; however, he may not fit all qualifications of the behaviorist. An attempt has been made here to classify theories according to their concerns for the principles of specific behavior as compared to more general concerns, especially in regard to the peripheral or central focus of psychological study.

The preceding theorists were not particularly concerned with perception, thinking, or individual meaning in describing behavior and learning. Their careful description of selected stimuli and responses made it unnecessary to postulate "thinking" activity.

In everyday language, the behavior of Thorndike's or Guthrie's cats could be described very differently. The naïve observer might say that Guthrie's cat wanted to get out of the box, that he perceived a relationship between his movement and the door opening, and that he walked out of the box when he saw that the door was open. Upon being again placed in the box, he saw the same situation and saw no reason for not acting the same way. This naïve observer might hypothesize that if the same movement did not work the next time, the cat would look for new methods of escape. Similarly, Skinner's pigeons might be described as recognizing that pecking in a certain way would produce food; this recognition controlled their behavior. Or, with Pavlov's dog, the bell came to mean or signify the potential presence of food, and salivation was the response to that expectation.

Another group of theorists would, in general, accept the statements of this naïve observer and be more concerned about the effects of

LEARNING THEORIES:
THE FIELD THEORISTS

6

perception, internal organization, and cognition as the determiners of action.

We might describe the major difference between the specifists and the other theorists in relation to the concept of mediation. To what extent are there intermediate processes between stimuli and response, between the external situation and the activity of the learner? The specifists prefer a model that uses a minimum of mediation, they find it more useful to postulate the establishment of a relatively direct connection between input and output. The common thing in all the other theories to be described is the postulation of mediating processes of some sort. In some cases, direct evidence of such mediation is sought. In others, mediation is inferred as necessary to a complete or accurate description. The mediation always takes the form of some sort of internal organization and its effects in governing the reception of the stimuli, their translation, and the way in which action results.

PERCEPTION, COGNITION, AND ACTION: the Field Theorists

THE GESTALTISTS

Starting with a middle European point of view, more affected by philosophical traditions and less enamored of the mechanical models of physical science, a group of German psychologists vociferously challenged the concepts identified with Thorndike and Watson. The men historically associated with this position are Wertheimer, Koffka, and Köhler (9, 11, 14, 15, 16, 17, 22, 32). The position they took was labeled Gestalt psychology (with a capital G in deference to German language conventions) because of their basic concern with perception, its patterns, its presumed dynamic organization, and its holistic character. The word "Gestalt" may be inadequately translated as a pattern, configuration, or self-regulating organized entity. It implies the priority of units larger than simple sensations and, psychologically, it implies that behavior is more than a simple addition of discrete units. The cliché that the whole is more than the sum of its parts derives from the organizational principle implicit in a Gestalt. The plural of the word is Gestalten, which has been carried over into English usage. The largest conceivable Gestalt is not made up of a synthesis of Gestalten but rather may be analyzed, for convenience, into smaller Gestalten whose characteristics may be partly accounted for by their membership in the larger Gestalt.

Philosophically, a thoroughgoing Gestaltist would perceive the physical world as well as human behavior in it as an organized Gestalt, made up of dynamically interrelated subsystems. Any change in one part will have its effect, to some extent, on the entire structure. This effect will not be one of simple addition or subtraction, but of a readjustment toward a re-established equilibrium.

In effect, said the Gestaltist to the behaviorist, "there are more things in heaven and earth than are dreamt of in your psychology." The unknown territory between the stimulus and the response is a major concern of the Gestaltists.

As compared with the positions already surveyed, the Gestaltists tend to be more concerned with complex relationships, central processes, and dynamic interactions than with specific movements or units of association.

Historically, Gestalt psychology began with phenomena of visual perception as a psychological problem. Why are a series of successive still pictures exposed at a particular rate seen as a moving picture? Why are a series of lights flashing on and off in a sequence perceived with a definite impression of movement, as if they were "chasing each other"? Why are these perceptions so coercive even after we know the facts? It is almost impossible to see a motion picture as a series of stills. Even if the timing of the presentation is bad, we will see it as moving "jerkily" but still moving.

Do you see this pattern as equal segments of black and white?

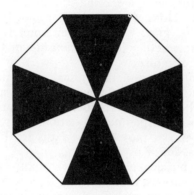

Most people do not. It is usually seen as a black cross. The white portion appears empty, less substantial than the black. By an effort of attention (or spontaneously for some), it may be shifted and seen as a white cross, in which case the white portions leap forward slightly and the black portions recede. For the Gestaltist, this cannot be explained as ·a mere summing up of sensations arising from the stimulus properties of the drawing. Nor can it be explained as a result of learning. It is more a *basis* for learning than a *result* of it.

This "figure-ground" characteristic was one of the first defined properties of a visual field. It illustrates the importance of organization and relationships in perception. Not only is organization seen as important; it is hypothesized that there is a congruence of organization in brain processes that makes the relationship more fundamental than the discrete sensations. As organisms, we are organized to see things in relationship.

I see a rectangular table top as rectangular, even though a mapping of retinal sensations would deny this. Seeing it as rectangular, I behave toward it as though it were and the behavior is successful. Unfortunately, there are also visual illusions that are not the way I see them. When I react toward them, the behavior may not work. I now use the new data to correct my understanding of the thing itself, and I am able to modify my behavior accordingly. To the Gestaltist, perception is primary and behavior is a response to the organization of the perceptual field.

Though we have used visual perception for illustration here, it must be remembered that there are many modes of perception interacting in a total perceptual field. The same broad principles of perception apply to the auditory, tactile, and kinaesthetic modes of perception and to their interaction.

Animal behavior is said to be guided by perception and some degree of symbolic process as is human behavior, although at a less complex, less elaborate level. In one demonstration, chickens were trained to peck grain from a dark gray paper and to avoid the grain on a light gray paper. Then a substitution was made: the dark gray paper was retained and an even darker gray was substituted for the lighter one. If the chickens had learned to peck in accord with a specific stimulus, they would have stuck to the original shade. However, they now avoided the dark gray and pecked from the darker gray. Gestaltists interpret this as an indication that the chickens were reacting to a *relationship* in the perceptual field, rather than to specific stimuli.

Among the most interesting of the animal experiments illustrating the Gestalt point of view are those described by Köhler in *The Mentality of Apes* (17). Between 1912 and 1917, Köhler was located on the island of Tenerife at an anthropoid experimental station, where his work with and observation of chimpanzees provided the basis for his book, which has become one of the classics of psychology.

Unlike the cats in puzzle boxes, Köhler's chimpanzees were observed in more naturalistic situations, though not in their native habitat. Controls were less rigorous, and the reports of activities are anecdotal and analytical rather than statistical. In this discussion, the terms "ape" and "chimpanzee" will be used interchangeably.

In the first place, Köhler found evidence that some of his chimpanzees learned more quickly and better than others. He also found that once the chimpanzee "saw" the relationships in a problem, his behavior toward it changed. Once he "saw" the solution to the problem, he immediately engaged in behavior appropriate to that solution. Blind trial and error occurred only when the solution was too difficult to be grasped by methods that appeared to be essentially perceptual and symbolic.

For most of the apes, for example, a box in the cage was an object to play with and sit on. However, when a banana was suspended from the ceiling of the cage too high for normal reaching or jumping, the animals looked for a way of getting to it. The box then became (was perceived as) a jumping stool. After this perceptual solution was reached, the action of dragging the box closer to the banana, climbing on it, and jumping for the banana came very quickly and efficiently. In some cases, the original proximity of the box to the banana helped with the solution. In others, an ape who had seen another employ this solution solved the problem similarly. Köhler contends that this last case involved not mere imitation of the activity, but an understanding of the solution and its application.

In a variation of this demonstration, the banana was placed higher and there was more than one box in the cage. Typically, the apes tried to use the one-box technique unsuccessfully. It seemed somewhat more difficult to perceive the possible efficacy of putting one box on top of another to achieve a higher jumping platform. Eventually this was done, but not as a stable structure. Rather, the second box was typically placed precariously on the other only long enough to launch the jump. Only the most intelligent of the apes seemed to achieve the concept of a stable two-box structure. None of them seemed able to effect a stable three-box structure. Hence, it is contended that differences in ability are important in determining the level of performance.

In one of the most quoted descriptions of the chimpanzees, Sultan, who is described as the most intelligent, was trying to reach a banana lying outside the cage. He extended his reach with a bamboo stick, quite a common activity. The stick was too short. Sultan engaged in a variety of activities, including throwing the stick at the fruit. This is obviously not a satisfactory solution in reality, but the need to make contact was so strong that this action seemed to be partially satisfying. Finally, he apparently gave up, turned his back on the banana, and started playing with two bamboo sticks. In his manipulation of them, he placed the smaller stick in the end of the larger one and made a double-length stick. He immediately returned to the banana problem and used his "new" stick to draw the banana into the cage. In similar later situations, this solution was repeated. Even when the two sticks fell apart, they were quickly rejoined. Having discovered this solution, Sultan even used his new tool to draw other objects into the cage. He seemed to enjoy the activity itself.

For the early Gestaltist, then, the prototype of learning was the perception of a situation, recognition of problematical aspects, solution by perceptual insights (either immediate or slowly developed), and action in terms of those insights. These behaviors are not isolated, they are part of the congruent organization of the physical and psychological worlds. This congruence is not complete, but it is close enough to permit agreements upon reality orientation.

KURT LEWIN

A student of the early Gestaltists, Lewin added some dimensions to learning theory that have tremendous implications for classroom teaching (11, 18, 19, 22, 32). For Lewin, as for other Gestaltists, behavior is a function of perception; however, he chooses to pay more attention to the external arrangements, the field to be perceived, than do the earlier theorists. Paradoxically, this leads to much concern with the subjective structuring of the field and to an analysis of the individual variables that contribute to the structuring. In this sense, Lewin is the first of the theorists discussed in these pages who leans toward personality theory as a necessary component of learning theory.

The cognitive field. The men who initiated the Gestalt theory tended to be preoccupied with specific phenomena perceived as whole situations and reacted to with behavior appropriate to that perception. These phenomena were seen as larger and more significant than simple stimuli and responses. In a similar expansion, Lewin sees these phenomena as parts of a larger Gestalt, composed of the cognitive field of the individual. In a sense, we perceive a particular phenomenon in terms of our understanding of its relationship to other organized phenomena that we already "know" or in accordance with its fit in the total way in which we organize our world. In particularly vivid, intense, or persistent experiencing of phenomena, we may find it necessary to reorganize our cognitive field or change our point of view. Yet, there is a persistence or a continuity in an individual's cognitive field that affects his perception of phenomena. It might be said that Lewin made thinking and the organization of knowing psychologically respectable again.

There is nothing mystical about Lewin's cognition. It is partly dependent upon field forces in the outside world and is, at any particular moment, dependent upon a dynamic interaction of those field forces and the existing cognitive field.

The life space. Each of us exists and acts in a world that we presume has common and identical features. We agree on the objective existence and nature of enough of those features to support the presumption. Yet, each of us has cognized the world somewhat differently, and at any given moment, we re-cognize it differently. At times, we act in ways that are inconsistent with our cognition of the real world. Lewin uses the term "life space" to refer to the psychological world each of us carries with us and in which we move. Our goals, values, wishes, and attitudes, as well as our cognitive field are all components of the life space. Some of us have quite restricted life spaces and are quite insensitive to many aspects of the world outside. Others have extended life spaces, which provide a broad compass of sensitivity to the world around us. Others have large components of fantasy in their life space, enabling either blocking out or severe distortion of perception of the outside world. Still others have a life space so congruent with reality that perceptions are by any available test clearcut reflections of the world outside, permitting objective realistic action in that world.

Vectors and barriers. There are psychologically immediate and more remote regions of the life space, with the more immediate having greater influence on our perception and overt behavior than the more remote. This idea of different regions gives rise to the notion of "vectors" or lines of force, resulting from the various internal and external pressures of and in the life space. Take, for example, the case of a college student living in a fraternity house. Let us say he has a well defined vocational goal of becoming a lawyer. There is an examination the next day that he perceives as an important step toward that goal. He further perceives the necessity of spending the evening studying in order to do well in the examination. At the same time, he is concerned with his immediate social relations with fellow fraternity members, and there are plans for evening activities that would interfere with his study. Furthermore, he perceives these plans as more attractive in themselves than the studying would be. His actual behavior would result from the relative force of these various pressures acting upon him. If he perceives the probability of actual failure in the exam and his vocational goal is quite important, he may do one thing. If he perceives that the social stigma of not joining in the activity will be great and that he will probably at least pass the exam, his behavior may be quite different. There are myriad possibilities of forces in many directions, and his behavior will be a result, or a vector, of the relative strengths of pushes and pulls in these various directions. In this same example, the examination may be seen as a barrier in his life space, a block between his present status and his goal. How will he handle this barrier? He may actually remove it by learning enough to pass the examination. He may see it as so insurmountable that he may change his goal. He may go around it by cheating in the examination. Any of these or other possible solutions would depend upon the vectors in his current life space.

Vectors are, of course, either positive or negative, with differing degrees of strength. It is conceivable that exactly opposite vectors of identical strength might cancel one another out, resulting in paralysis of behavior. Actually, this kind of balance is seldom achieved (except in severe neuroses); the actual behavior we engage in may be represented by the deflection of the conflicting forces in a vector, which is the dynamic resultant of the conflict.

For Lewin, then, human behavior is the direct result of vectors in the current life space. The past and the future are both represented in the present, but it is their current force that makes the difference. It is probable that a past-oriented person will grant greater force to tradition, previous learnings, and things known to be true; a future-oriented person will respond more to the force of goals, expectations, and future possibilities.

Apparently, little has been said so far about learning. We have been talking about behavior rather than changes in it or changes in the person that result in changes in it. This is typical of Lewinian thinking, in that the situation and the individual's perception and cognition of it control his behavior. Cognition, here, includes the idea of predictions of outcomes or estimates of the results of behavior. It should be evident that learning is perceived as problem solving, seeking the perceptions that will restructure the cognitive field, acting in ways that will overcome barriers, and incorporating these understandings and ways of behaving into the newly reorganized life space.

Characteristically, much of the research and theorizing of the Lewinian point of view has been done under the heading of motivation. One of the more important considerations in the life space has been the self-concept, the "who am I?" Implicit in this consideration is the estimate of development—"who am I to become?"

Level of aspiration. One aspect of the self-concept that has stimulated considerable research in learning is the level of aspiration. This may be defined in operational terms as expected performance that will make an individual feel successful. The congruence of or discrepancy between actual performance and aspirational level is one of the sources of tension in the person and carries a great deal of motivational value. Some people tend to set their goals excessively high and are under constant pressure to achieve more than is reasonable. Others set their goals so low that they are seldom under this kind of pressure, being easily able to meet the demands they put on themselves. These people probably achieve less than they could. The third possibility is obviously a realistic goal-setting tendency, in which the level of aspiration is compatible with achievement possibilities.

Typical experiments in level of aspiration assign a series of tasks to individuals, asking them to set their goals on each task. Successes and failures are built into the experimental design. A record is kept of the individual's changing goal-setting tendencies in the light of patterns of success and failure. Obviously, the individual must be sufficiently ego-involved in the task to take it seriously. There are subtle effects in the results produced by different arrangements; however, in general, it has been found that continued success leads to realistic goal setting while failure may lead to three possible reactions: (1) The lowering of the level of aspiration so that a subjective effect of failure is minimized. (2) The raising of the aspiration in the face of failure so that the individual puts more pressure on himself. (3) The individual's withdrawal from the situation (leaving the field).

Another area of investigation that has grown out of field theory is the whole area of group dynamics, the influence of others and of group membership on the behavior of individuals. Much of this work has been assimilated into general psychology, social psychology, and sociology and is mentioned here to indicate the importance of field theory in generating ideas.

EDWARD C. TOLMAN

Tolman may be considered a "Field-Behaviorist" in that his origins and methods are behavioristic and follow the experimental traditions of behaviorist schools (11, 32, 33, 34). Yet, his interpretation of results, the hypotheses he makes, and his way of thinking about behavior and learning are more consistent with field and Gestalt theory. In his later work, Tolman expressed his indebtedness to Lewin and saw a close relationship between Lewin's concept of the life space and his concept of the sign-Gestalt field and cognitive maps.

In the behaviorist tradition, most of Tolman's experimental work has been with laboratory rats and their maze behavior. His data came from objective, nonverbal, controlled animal behavior. His method is rigorously experimental. His interpretation of the data, however, uses such explanatory principles as insight, cognition, meaning, perception, field, and Gestalt. Rather than denying insight to man, Tolman ascribes insight to rats and explains their behavior in a maze as partly governed by cognition derived from perception.

In running a maze, a rat is certainly exposed to the stimuli of that maze; his responses are certainly related to those stimuli. But the process and significance of the stimuli and the resulting responses are a matter of cognition rather than direct conditioning. In perceiving and running the maze, a "cognitive map" or "field map" of the environment is formed, with certain features of the environment *selected* as guides or signs to the configuration of the map. These features of the environment *mean* the whole situation, they are significant of *means* to anticipated ends. The rat is goal directed. He is seen as having purposes in the maze. He learns *meanings*, the relation between behavior and an anticipated goal, rather than automatic movements in response to specific stimuli or activity reinforced retroactively by reward as Guthrie or Hull, respectively, would imply. This interpretation involves the "sign-Gestalt" concept in that the features of the maze become signs the rat recognizes as signifying the structure of the map. These signs provide the basis for acting within the situation.

Tolman is cautious about extending his observations of rats to human learning; however, the inference is reasonable that human beings similarly establish cognitive maps with ends-means qualities. With us, such maps are probably more complex and comprehensive because of the expansion of our language behavior.

Learning and performance. Tolman makes an important distinction between learning and performance. Technically, we can never observe learning; we can only observe performance and infer learning from it. We may define learning in terms of performance, but the actuality is not so simple. Performance may improve and additional learnings may be involved that continue to improve performance, but learning to do something may occur in the absence of observable performance. Changes in cognitive maps may occur, and only later be utilized in overt behavior.

Variables in the learning process. Even the simplest learning is complex. Tolman postulates a variety of intervening variables between the complex stimulus situation and the learned response even for a rat in a simple maze. The specific behavior of a rat (and presumably of other organisms) may be described as determined by the interaction of independent variables, which give rise to intervening variables, which, in turn, determine the actual behavior. More specifically, the independent variables are seen as two types, the environmental and the individual difference variables. The individual difference variables are described as heredity, age, previous training, and special conditions of endocrine, drug, or vitamin factors. These four sets of individual difference (H.A.T.E.) act upon each of the environmental variables to produce conditions in the organism, referred to as intervening variables, which directly affect behavior. Tolman defines six environmental variables and their corresponding parallels (33, pp. 144-78):

1. Maintenance schedules or the drive conditions of the organism are influenced by H.A.T.E. to produce *demand*.
2. Appropriate goal objects available to satisfy the drive result in *appetite*.
3. The stimuli provided in the situation produce *differentiation or the significant signs in the cognitive map.*
4. The types of motor responses required in the situation result in the application of *motor skills*.
5. The general pattern of the environmental situation is affected by H.A.T.E. to result in *biases in favor of one kind of behavior or another*.
6. Past and immediate experiences with ends-means behavior result in *hypotheses about the appropriate behavior to try in this situation*.

It may be suggested that the heart of the learning process is summed up in item 6. That is, the organism hypothesizes that certain behavior will be appropriate in this particular situation and engages in that behavior as a result of the hypothesis. The hungry rat will develop certain appetites that may assuage the hunger, will differentiate stimuli in the situation that may lead him to food, will marshall appropriate motor skills to his service, will use his biases in perceiving the situation, and will hypothesize that a certain line of behavior will be successful. Then, the specific behavior takes place.

Tolman presents experimental evidence that rats seek out appropriate stimuli, that they are not only passively affected by the situation. He also presents evidence of searching behavior of a vicarious trial-and-error kind. The rat may not need to actually run the maze, he may estimate the effect of certain potential behavior. It is contended that a survey of the situation is made, that a hypothesis is made concerning the best behavior for achieving the anticipated goal object, and that the verification of the hypothesis completes the learning process.

This may seem like a very complicated description of a rat's behavior in deciding to turn right or left in a maze. However, as a prototype of learning, it does emphasize the complexity of even the simplest behavior.

PHENOMENOLOGY: THE PERCEPTUAL FIELD AND INDIVIDUAL BEHAVIOR

The classification of theories in this section may be somewhat arbitrary. It was difficult to classify this theory because it has close relationships with both the Gestalt theories and with the personality theories of the next section. It was classified here because of its fundamental stress on perception as the determiner of behavior and learning.

Combs and Snygg are taken as the spokesmen for the point of view here presented (4). The perceptual concerns of the Gestaltists, Lewin's concept of the individual life space, and Tolman's cognitive maps and individual difference variables are taken as matters of the most central importance in phenomenology. According to the phenomenologists, the objective S of the theories we have called "specifist" is of relatively little importance, because the actual behavior of the individual depends upon his interpretation, his perception, his experiencing of the S. The perception of any particular S is embedded in the perceptual field of the individual and affects him only in that context. We behave as we perceive. Behavior, and the aspect of it called "learning," can be understood only in terms of the psychological reality of the individual as he perceives the phenomena affecting him. The meaning he ascribes to a situation gets into his perception of it, and he behaves in terms of this perception.

Learning as differentiation. Learning is seen as the process by which one changes his behavior. Since behavior is a function of the perceptual field at any given moment, differentiation within the perceptual field is the basis of learning. The fundamental Gestalt distinction between figure and ground is accepted and applied as a very broad principle. Differentiation is the process of clarifying and making precise those significant aspects of a situation that were formerly vague, unclear, or part of the "ground."

Learning is an active process and a function of need. The individual's need is one of the primary determiners of what he will differentiate and how he will act as he perceives the potential satisfaction of need. What we perceive ourselves as needing determines what we will learn. The intensity and level of need affects learning as well as the opportunities for differentiation that are available both externally and internally. First perceptions are gross and relatively undifferentiated. We differentiate and reorganize our perceptual field to satisfy the needs that are most pressing at the moment.

Habitual responses are those that result from low-level perceptions in the field. They are actions that have been reduced from a figure value to a ground value and are no longer central in our perception.

The perceptual point of view appears to be diametrically opposed to the S-R approach to learning, with which began our look at learning theories. Where the early behaviorists seemed to take perception for granted and to concentrate on specific stimuli and responses, the phenomenologists take the stimuli and responses as given and focus their concern upon the perceptual process by which stimuli are related and interpreted to give rise to meaningful responses.

It is evident from the discussion in Chapter 6
that the concerns for life space, self-concept,
individual difference variables, and the
individual perceptual field relate learning to
the personality of the learner. The increasing
concern with motivation and learning also
implies the need to look at the motivation
concepts that come from personality theory.
At this stage in psychology, this area is not
adequately related to learning theory.
However, it may be worthwhile to
try to find some of the relationships.

BEING AND BEHAVIOR: the Personality Theorists

Personality theory is a whole field in itself
and we will deal with other aspects of it as we
look at human growth and development
in Part Three of this volume. For now,
certain aspects of personality theory that may
throw light on learning have been selected.

SIGMUND FREUD

In a very real sense, any discussion of personality
theory in the twentieth century must make
Freud a reference point (3, 5, 9, 27). The
Freudian concepts of 1900, novel and sometimes

LEARNING THEORIES:
PERSONALITY
AND MOTIVATION

7

shocking at that time, have evolved and attained common currency today, at least in American culture. As a result, they have become basic to later theorizing to the extent that other theories may be appraised according to their adherence to or deviation from Freudian doctrine. Sometimes the technical disagreements as to details among theorists obscure the very basic foundation established by this point of view.

Psychoanalysis began with Freud's concern for patients whose difficulties were neither adequately explained nor adequately treated by the neurology of his time. His early theorizing attempted to develop new neurological models, soon moved to the direct influence of sexual behavior, and eventually to a more indirect and symbolic use of sexual material as a base for both explanation and therapy.

Analysis became both a source of data for explaining human behavior and a technique of therapy. Although Freud did not use learning terminology, therapy might be considered a process of changing the behavior of patients through changing the inner dynamics of their personalities. The process of free association, of verbalizing and interpreting whatever "comes to mind," became the research method and the "teaching method." Later analyses of the dynamics of therapy carry fascinating implications for teaching and learning.

The unconscious. One of the basic contributions of Freudian theory was its recognition of the importance of unconscious processes—those aspects of the person of which he is unaware. Much of our behavior and learning is governed by forces we normally do not recognize. Indeed, not only is much of our unconscious material and activity unavailable to consciousness, but much of our energy is devoted to keeping it that way. Hence, many of our conscious activities and much of our overt behavior stem both from unconscious factors and from the need to keep them unconscious. Under normal conditions, introspection into our motives will leave much hidden. Any complete description of behavior must include the unconscious aspects.

Libido. The reservoir of energy, the basis of motivation, the source of drives to activity is known as "libido." Sexual in origin, this energy is forced into channels of behavior that appear quite remote from sexual activity. Whether specifically correct or not, this insistence on energy source and a process by which it becomes attached to certain interests and activities is a fundamental contribution to learning theory.

Development stages. Concepts of the development of readiness for learning particular things as the child grows have become increasingly important in educational theory. Freudian theory of psychosexual stages of development has contributed both generally and specifically to this area. There are appropriate and inappropriate times for introducing activities and concepts, depending upon the individual's interests, needs, and particular stage of development. The school-age child, for example, is ready to learn some of the things the school demands, not only because of his accumulated experience and physical growth, but also because of the dynamic forces that have brought him to the psychosexual stage referred to as "latency." The resolution of earlier conflicts now enables him to turn his attention to the larger world outside his home and to work at the skills, knowledge, and other behavior required by the larger society. The specifics of conflict resolution partially govern individual differences in readiness for learning.

The specific theory of psychosexual development will be dealt with in a later discussion of personality development.

Personality structure. If there are conscious and unconscious processes, if there are libidinal energies, and if there are stages of development, there must be some sort of organization of the person whereby these aspects function. In his early theorizing, Freud attempted to describe neurological features that would serve these functions. Increasingly, he shifted to psychological descriptions and eventually developed a concept of personality "structure" that has been most useful in providing ways to talk about the psychological person. These concepts of id, ego, and superego carry implications for differential activity in learning.

This description of these phases of personality does not follow classical Freudian presentation with strict exactness. It is rather an interpretation of current usage of the terms, as derived from the development of psychoanalytic theory.

The id is originally the system of biological drives, energy, rudimentary instincts, and tendencies to act that forms the psychological equipment of the new-born child. Its characteristics change in some respects with increasing maturity of the organism. The id is characterized by tissue needs that demand satisfaction and by the development of bodily tensions that seek release. These satisfactions and releases provide gratification and pleasure; their denial provides frustration and pain. Based on what Freud called the "pleasure principle," the id seeks impulse gratification without regard for consequences other than its own libidinal expression. This is the source of basic drive or energy.

In adapting to social life, even in the first days of existence, the undisciplined gratification of the id cannot continue. Much of the child's gratification must come from care by others. Food, warmth, and protection are provided by parents, other adults, and external surroundings. This realization and the attaching of importance to the attitudes of others imposes the necessity of controlling some of the actions of the id. Consequently, the ego develops and fulfills the function of mediating between the id and outside forces. The "reality principle" of giving up immediate pleasures for long-range satisfaction governs the ego. In applying this principle, it rechannels the impulses of the id, suppressing some and permitting others in socially acceptable directions. It maintains contact between the id and external reality. In adult life, the ego generally is that part of ourselves of which we are conscious, including our concept of ourselves.

Yet, we cannot constantly deal consciously with every phenomenon of reality and make discrete decisions about every act. Many of our decisions about right and wrong must become automatic. Many of our desires and impulses are not dealt with on a conscious level by the ego. Certain libidinal desires are not acceptable to parents or society. The incidents whereby the child learns such restrictions are repressed to the unconscious mind, but a body of automatic commands and prohibitions associated with them remain as a governing phase of the personality called the "superego." What we usually term conscience is a function of the superego. Certain regulating attitudes are enforced by the superego, which indicates to the ego the presence of unacceptable desires by making the ego feel fear, shame, disgust, or other inhibiting emotions. Thus, the ego bears the brunt of the conflict between the id and superego.

The balancing of these phases of the personality—their continuous dynamic adjustment—provides a very complex pattern of motivation, which certainly affects the learning process. The ego tendency to seek clear perceptions of reality may easily be distorted by id impulses and superego demands. An individual's ability to learn and his focus of attention upon particular learning will be affected by his personality structure.

This picture of the personality indicates that the person learns to become what he is. Once having become what he is, he has developed ways of learning that will have some consistency and persistence. He has built into himself certain values and ways of reacting to the world. Psychological self-defense will affect what he can learn and how he can learn it. His behavior is inevitably influenced by the dynamic pressures of his unconscious wishes and fears, his ego defenses, and the ways he has learned to handle them.

Since Freud's original formulation there have been many developments and specific changes in details of psychoanalytic theory. We are not concerned with these details here, but primarily with the import of the general approach as it carries implications for describing how we learn.

HENRY A. MURRAY

There are many personality theories that use the concept of "needs." Perhaps one of the most influential of these systems, in terms of defining the area, giving impetus to research and writing, and influencing later thinking, has been Murray's theory (21). Murray's concepts have a great deal of affinity with Freudian and Gestalt theory. The system is essentially a descriptive one with inferences as to the source of behavior coming from the relationships in the description. There are two major terms that may be used to discuss the system as it relates to learning: "press" and "needs."

Press. Murray conceives of the existence of a real world that produces stimuli capable of affecting the organism. These situational factors are referred to as the "alpha press" or the objective and primary pressures outside the organism. This idea is similar to Lewin's "physical environment" or Koffka's "geographical environment." More important psychologically is the "beta press," which corresponds to Lewin's perceptions of the life space or Koffka's "phenomenological environment." Stimulating conditions in the external situation receive attention and affect the individual according to the momentary organization of his system of needs.

This idea is familiar from the previous discussions of perception. It again emphasizes both the continuity and discontinuity of the psychological and the physical environment. To illustrate this, Murray's analysis of the common press of childhood includes the press of danger or misfortune (p. Danger or Misfortune). An accident of some sort to the child would be a possible event in this category. There must be some sort of an occurrence (alpha press) that the child can perceive as having some signifi-

cance. The way in which he perceives it, the way it affects him, its importance or lack of importance (beta press) will depend upon the needs
he has at the time of its occurrence. Thus, a relatively minor accident
might be extremely important to one child, and not even noticed by another, depending upon the dynamic balance of the need to avoid harm
(n. Harmavoidance) with other needs in the personality.

Needs. Like many other constructs in psychological theory, needs may
not be known directly but may only be inferred from other behavior.
Systems deriving from Murray use the concept of manifest need as a way
of dealing with this difficulty. In other words, these theories do not say
that there is necessarily a need, for example, for aggression. In research,
they ask the question, does the individual behave in such a way that we
might describe his behavior as attributable to a need for aggression? What
kind of behavior do we see that manifests some dynamic that might be
referred to as a need for aggression?

Needs theories of this type postulate that certain observable behaviors
can be described as exhibiting manifest needs. These manifest needs may,
in turn, be postulated as being the result of latent needs. It is obvious
that the life history of the individual would eventually be necessary to
validate the specifics of such an analysis. The outcome of development,
following a theory similar to the Freudian theory, would result in a
complex of latent needs, which would be relatively persistent in the individual. This complex would be one of the factors determining the specific
beta press that would provide the individual's psychological potential for
behavior. The resultant behavior would show manifest needs, from which
the observer could infer latent needs and other aspects of the personality.

This general approach is not essentially different from Freudian theory
or other approaches that postulates the development of some sort of a
needs structure, which provides the motivational system for an individual.
The unique values of Murray's theory lie in his peculiar identification of
needs, which seems to include both the lack and the potential satisfiers.
Among those that have stimulated additional research and discussion and
seem to give the flavor of Murray's thinking are the following:

1. n. Affiliation: producing behavior that leads to friendliness, to seeking out others to associate with, to becoming part of a group or
   a movement, to seeking ways of associating with others.

2. n. Deference: shown by behavior compliant to others, devotion,
   suggestibility, etc.

3. n. Nurturance: manifest in taking care of others, being kind, seeking ways to show concern for fellow human beings.

4. n. Harmavoidance: realistically present for all normal people, shown
   in excess as extreme timidity, fearfulness, specific worries about
   dangers.

5. n. Blameavoidance: shown by extreme ego-protective behavior, ration-
   alization, behavior that expunges guilt.

6. n. Abasement: in some ways the opposite of n. Blameavoidance,
   shown by surrender to ascription of inferiority, acceptance of
   blame, seeking a subservient position.

7. n. Aggression: shown in temper outbursts, combative behavior, destruction of things.

8. n. Dominance: shown in behavior that dominates others, coercion, recognized leadership.

9. n. Noxavoidance: in normal degrees—the avoidance of noxious substances, in extremes—hypersensitive behavior, for example, extreme concern about foods, poisonous substances, etc.

10. n. Achievement: manifest in striving behavior, in mastery, in control of actual forces.

11. n. Recognition: shown by seeking the praise of others, performing to receive fame, etc.

12. n. Order: manifest in cleanliness, orderliness, finickiness about detail.

From this brief listing, it will be clear that these identifications are descriptive dimensions, ways of talking about human motivation. Many other terms have also been used by Murray and others as labels for describing the sources of individual behavior. It should also be apparent that each of these needs might be seen as a continuum along which we might portray the common qualities underlying behavior, as well as the differential balances of particular individuals.

Carrying this particular kind of needs theory into its implications for teaching and learning, it provides a way of organizing our thinking about individuals, a basis for setting hypotheses and following through on evaluation. The drives to action implicit in a person high in n. Achievement and n. Recognition will be quite different from those in a person high in n. Blameavoidance and n. Order. Differential treatment of such individuals will be necessary if particular outcomes of learning are expected.

The preceding treatment of Murray's approach to needs theory is far from complete. Being a descriptive system, different situations bring different descriptions. There are a variety of formulations of specific needs. This treatment has included only those that seem generally meaningful to serve as illustrations of the position.

ABRAHAM MASLOW

Unlike Murray's descriptive approach, there are needs theories that imply values, development, and degrees of adequacy of behavior. Increasingly influential in this area is the concept of a hierarchy of needs as developed by Maslow (1, 20).

Most of the learning theories and needs theories presented so far have assumed inadequacies. They have assumed that there is something lacking, that motivation consists of some kind of imbalance, tension, or distress. We learn either as an attempt to satisfy, or as a result of satisfying, the lack. Even in such "minimal motivational" themes as Guthrie's, this is true to some extent.

Carried to its logical conclusions, such an approach would imply that once equilibrium, balance, or satisfaction has been achieved, there is no more learning or behavior. Again, logically, this difficulty is overcome by assuming (with considerable evidence to support the assumption) that environmental pressures are such that equilibrium is only fleetingly, if ever, attained.

Parallel with this generally accepted position has developed a rejection of the idea of "instincts" as applied to man and the more complex mammals. Despite Freud's use of "instinctual" drive or energy, the acceptable concept was essentially a biological organismic one that rejected the usual interpretation of instinct. In recent years, instinct has been typically defined as a relatively complex set of behaviors engaged in without having to be learned (as we have defined learning). Certainly, lower animals show a considerable amount of behavior that is instinctive in this sense. In man, practically no observable behavior can fit this description. Under food deprivation, we become hungry and seek to eat, but the seeking behavior, the eating behavior, and the necessary concomitants are so highly variable and so subject to learning experiences that they cannot meet the definition of instinct. The possibilities of specific behavior are limited only by the physical and biological characteristics of the organism, not by any pre-set series of activities, which might be called "instinctive."

Allied with this quite correct observation, a general tendency has developed to eliminate completely any notion of instinct in human psychology and to substitute a conception of the biological organism with a minimum of prepotent tendencies, these given by the sheer necessity of biological maintenance. The one major exception to this has been those theories of the Freudian type, which saw energies and drives as "instinctual"—not full-fledged instinctive behavior.

As a result of this logical and historical development, psychologists have become wary of recurrent attempts to resurrect the concept of instinct. However, there are increasing numbers of thinkers in various fields who are unsatisfied with the minimal assumptions about human nature, who require more positive forces than mere survival of the organism, and who perceive a hierarchy of human needs as motivation toward a state of being that is more than equilibrium or surcease from external pressure. Among these thinkers, a highly modified concept of instinct is gaining currency.

Maslow postulates that each of us has an essential inner nature—"given," "natural"—that includes needs he call "instinctoid." These needs are in no sense to be interpreted as instinctive behavior in the conventional sense; they are remnants of instincts, which set a potential for growth and behavior favoring certain directions over others and providing the bases for motivations that are naturally more "healthy" than "unhealthy." These directions of behavior are, to some extent, prior to experience.

We cannot easily imagine a world in which human nature can operate without frustrations. Hence, it is meaningless to speculate about such a situation. Realistically, some frustrations provided by physical reality provide the scene whereby human nature tests itself and is able to develop its potential. On the other hand, to the extent that it is possible, satisfaction is more growth-producing than frustration because of the inherent growth potential of the organism.

It is common in many theories to speak of "growth." In the developmental years, prior to maturity, this is a common-sense idea. Followed by analogy into physical maturity, it is still common to speak of growth toward some concept of psychological maturity. As long as we are "becoming" something, we can use the concept of growth. It is more difficult to think of "being" as an active process. Most psychologies assume a basis for motivation that is limited to growth or maintenance. Maslow goes beyond this in postulating energies put to use in enhancing "being" in a way that is beyond mere maintenance. He applies this idea to both needs and levels of cognition.

Becoming and being. With other need theorists, Maslow perceives one aspect of needs as involving the removal of deficiencies, as finding ways to provide satisfactions that are lacking. To a large extent, the seeking to remove deficiencies, the attempt to overcome frustrations, the search for satisfaction of unmet needs provide the motivation for learning, for becoming someone different who is able to act in different ways. These motivations are referred to as deficiency needs (*D*-needs) or needs generated by some conflict between the growing person and the environmental press. Cognition (as in Murray's beta press) is usually the response to such deficiency orientation (*D*-cognition). Much of our development and actual learning may be ascribed to the motivation coming from *D*-needs and mediated by *D*-cognitions.

The unusual aspects of Maslovian theory go beyond this deficiency orientation to postulate *B*-cognition or a true perception—interpretation of the thing or event *per se* without reference to distortion by deficiency needs. By the nature of things in the contemporary world, this seldom happens. It is, however, one of the ultimate stages of maturity when things or events can actually be perceived as they are or, to use Murray's terminology, when alpha and beta press become "one."

This concept of *D*-needs and *B*-needs is perhaps one of the most important contributions of the Maslovian point of view. It is certainly one of the most controversial. The idea grows directly out of the concept of "instinctoid" human nature, namely, that when deficiencies are satisfied, when there are no longer deprivations, there are still motivating forces in the individual, stemming from the very nature of his being. For the definition of motivation used in this volume, Maslow's language becomes difficult at this point. He sometimes talks about unmotivated behavior and uses the term "motivation" to refer only to the effects of deficiency needs. In the context of our discussion, it is more appropriate to use the equally common language of *D*-motivation and *B*-motivation, implying different but equally valid motivational processes.

The preceding discussion is a rather extended introduction to provide a context for the hierarchical needs system that is the organizing principle of Maslovian theory. Each of the needs contains some elements of both *D*-orientation and *B*-orientation. However, the higher we go in the hierarchy, the greater the influence of *B*-orientation as we move closer to psychological maturity.

The needs. It is customary to discuss the Maslovian hierarchy from the most immature to the most mature needs. With our previous introduction to concepts of "being," it may be interesting to reverse the process and look at the higher-order needs first, moving down the hierarchy to the earliest and most primitive.

1. The self-actualization need. At the highest levels of psychological maturity, the individual has a need to be himself, to act in a manner

73

consistent with who he is. This implies developing one's potential, becoming and being whatever one is capable of. If all other needs are essentially satisfied, this need still operates and provides the ultimate motivations. The person then operates primarily on B-motivations rather than being pressured by D-motivations. This level makes possible true objectivity—dealing with the world as it is, rather than with distortions stemming from deficiency needs.

It is difficult to communicate a clear picture of behavior at the self-actualization level, because so few of us reach it. Its qualities are beyond our usual experience. Maslow studied a number of people who seemed to operate at this level and found some rather interesting variations from the usual descriptions of average human behavior. It is his contention that perhaps only 1 per cent of the population achieve consistent operation at the self-actualization level.

On the other hand, if we look at our own experiences, we will find moments (or perhaps longer periods of time) when all of our other needs seem to be satisfied and we are free to do what we "really want" to do without regard to coping with everyday pressures. There may be moments when everything happens right and we get a glimmer of what it is like to be a complete person with a feeling of self-fulfillment. At these rare times, we approach or achieve self-actualization. Truly creative behavior is evidence of this level.

This need is present in all of us. It emerges as a major factor only when lower-level needs are routinely satisfied. Being present, however, it can operate as a deficiency need for those who are consistently operating on a lower level. A person seeking prestige or one operating at the level of safety needs will still attempt to perform in a way consistent with his self-concept. To the extent that he knows himself, his mode of behavior will be consistent with eventual self-actualization. Under extreme pressures, this may not be true because some degree of satisfaction at lower levels must be present for higher needs to emerge.

2. The esteem needs. Prepotent to self-actualization is the need for esteem. Until we are assured that we are respected by others and can build self-respect, our behavior will be dominated by attempts to do so. We will look for evidences of the respect of others and engage in activities presumed to win that respect, even to doing things that constitute violations of our self-concept. The desire to be famous, to be recognized as important, to be the big man on campus may be motivated by these needs. The self-actualizing person appreciates the respect of others, may accept fame as it comes to him, but he doesn't *need* it. For him, prestige and fame may be by-products of being himself; they have ceased to be motivational because they were routinely satisfied and have lost their potency.

3. Love and belonging needs. Esteem needs cannot emerge until the more basic needs for love, affection, and belonging are satisfied. The person must be assured that he is loved, that he is a worthy person, that he is acceptable because he is accepted. Severe frustration at this level is responsible for some of the more bizarre behavior in psychological literature and everyday life. Failure to distinguish that these needs are basic and pre-

potent to the esteem needs creates some of our greatest problems in handling children. Many teachers say to children, in effect, "I will love you if you achieve," thus tying an esteem level behavior to the love need. As a result, the child may try to buy love by acting as though he wanted to achieve. Neither behavior really works. Love needs demand unconditional acceptance as a relatively consistent thing in order to move on to the next stage.

4. The safety needs. The individual cannot seek or give love until he feels relatively safe from harm, danger, or threat of destruction. He must find ways to live in a relatively secure world before he is free to do other things. This is true in regard to actual danger of physical harm and also in regard to a need for regularity, for some predictability about the way the world operates. Probably many of our basic cognitive needs arise from this level. Our efforts to understand, to make sense of the world, are partly motivated by safety needs. Many people cannot respond to a love relationship because they need to protect themselves against the potential dangers of letting down barriers. Persons motivated by safety needs are likely to restrict themselves, to retreat under threat, and to be intolerant of ambiguity. The world is too threatening a place in which to move without armor and defenses.

Only the person who has early learned that the world is relatively safe and that he is able to defend himself against real dangers can be free enough for high levels of development.

5. The physiological needs. Basic to all life is the need to maintain the physical organism. Under severe deprivation of food and temperature control or under the threat of noxious or destructive conditions, the person needs to protect his physical and physiological being. All needs theories start at this level and tend to perceive it as basic and prepotent. The person who is truly on the edge of starvation will be dominated by food-seeking behavior and food symbols. His perception will be narrowed and restricted to a field dominated by nourishment needs.

With these basic needs prepotent, it is difficult to explain the many cases in which an individual denies himself food so others may have it or voluntarily goes on a hunger strike to the point of no return. It is presumed that in these cases the individual has reached a higher need level with such security that the higher need has achieved autonomy and is incapable of being overcome by needs that were once prepotent. A careful analysis of the individual need structure would be necessary for a full explanation.

This point leads us to the concept of the dual nature of needs as developmental and as operative after the developmental period. In developing to maturity, we go through the needs in sequence, a higher-level need emerging only as lower-level needs are essentially satisfied. Complete satisfaction is not necessary, and there will be evidence of higher-level needs while one is still operating primarily at the lower levels. Severe deprivation at any level will retard or make impossible the emergence of the next level. In a mature personality, all of the needs are still present but the personality is increasingly dominated by higher-level needs. Under threat of deprivation, one may move down the scale and become dominated by lower-level needs. However, it is important to note that the more completely one is operating at higher levels, the more one is insulated against threat at the lower levels. For the self-actualizing person, the threat to safety needs must be very real and very intense for him to violate his self-actualization need. He will usually find ways to protect himself that are consistent with self-actualization. For the person who consistently operates at or near the safety-needs level, such threat need not be as real or as intense before it causes an almost total mobilization of the personality. In common-sense terms, a timid person may be terrified of his own shadow while a secure person can face real danger with a minimum of fear.

Basic and manifest needs. One other aspect of this theory requires attention, the concept of basic and manifest needs. A person may act as if he were motivated by love needs, for example, when he is actually using this behavior to try to satisfy safety needs. We have already noted that we encourage children to use esteem behavior as a substitute for the satisfaction of love needs. The manifest behavior then may be a symptom of unmet lower needs even though it appears to stem from a higher need. Such behavior is never satisfactory, never appropriate to the real satisfaction of needs. The person who seeks the esteem of his fellow man as a substitute for unmet love needs or as a way of finding safety is not satisfied by the esteem, even if he receives it, because it is not what he is really seeking. Manifest behavior must be appropriate to the need it seeks to satisfy before the individual can satisfy that need and move on to the higher level.

OTHER ASPECTS OF NEEDS THEORIES

Additional needs theories will be discussed in Part Three as a way of looking at children's growth, development, and behavior. The extended treatment given to Maslow's theoretical position has set the stage for more practical applications in that section. There are, however, two additional theorists, consistent with the Maslovian conceptualization, who can add to our understanding (1, 4, 24).

Combs has already been mentioned in the discussion of perception and learning. He also makes a contribution to needs theory through a simplification of the hierarchy of needs. Combs contends that we can reduce the fundamental and continuing motivation to a *need for personal adequacy.* This implies that all of our activities are motivated by a drive to develop, maintain, and enhance our perceived self as adequate under the circumstances of life. Seen in this light, Maslow's hierarchy is a useful breakdown of aspects of this need and a description of various possible stages of its application. Thus, safety, love, and esteem are areas in which the individual develops and expresses the need for personal adequacy. Self-actualization is an ultimate stage, where most of the threat and defense no longer need to be coped with and the enhancement phase of personal adequacy is dominant. This concept may be useful as an organizing principle that ties together many diversified theories.

Carl Rogers uses the phrase "a fully functioning person" to say something similar to Combs's concept. Where Freud's theories developed through work with relatively severely neurotic patients and Maslow's concepts were tested on a rare level of presumedly healthy subjects, Rogers' work and theoretical development has been forged in contact with an intermediate group of relatively normal people with problems and some degree of conflict.

Rogers is identified with "nondirective," or "client-centered" therapy, which some writers have identified as a rediscovery of Freudian free association. This is not entirely true, because specific techniques are involved that differ markedly from the techniques of psychoanalysis.

In Rogerian therapy, the client's statements are accepted; he may say whatever he wishes. The therapist's function is to provide a setting that will encourage uninhibited verbal expression and to honestly reflect the feelings of the client. In general, the therapist is not interested in the content of what the patient says. He certainly is not interested in criticizing or censoring it. He is interested in using the material to reflect the feelings of the client, to help him accept his feelings and move on to a more adequate perception of the world and his behavior in it. Through this process, the client perceives more clearly, accepts himself and life as it is, and is enabled to become a person better able to cope with the real world. He becomes a more fully functioning person.

The assumptions underlying such a process are essentially optimistic in the Maslovian sense. Human nature is trustworthy. Given a chance, the individual will do those things that are right for his own development and optimal functioning. Given a chance to express, accept, and integrate his feelings and concomitant perceptions, the individual will move toward "self-fulfillment," "full functioning," "personal adequacy," or "self-actualization." Implicit in these points of view is the idea that, in the long run, such functioning will be appropriate in serving the needs of other people and the conditions of the world.

These theories of being and behaving carry tremendous implications for teaching. Unlike the usual concept of the teacher setting the goal and controlling the pupil in order to move him to that goal, we have here the implication that the teacher may trust the pupil. He may accept, as at least momentarily necessary, the pupil's own perceptions and goals. He may depend upon growth forces in the individual to move him in appropriate directions. He does not have to "motivate" the pupil. Motivation is already there. The teacher's job is to find and provide situations that will tap the individual's positive motivations and make possible the kind of growth of which he is capable.

To supplement the systematic theories of learning, three additional approaches will be considered: physiological correlates of learning, empirical findings about learning, and a broad classification of types of learning, all of which cut across the theoretical positions.

PHYSIOLOGICAL AND NEUROLOGICAL ASPECTS

It should be clear that any complete description of learning must eventually describe the inner changes of the organism in terms of physiological functioning (10, 35, 36). What changes take place in the body functioning, in the endocrine glands, in various body systems? It is commonly agreed that the total organism learns, but that the focus of learning activity is probably centered in the brain and nervous system. How does this neural network operate to permit learning and how does it maintain the learning that has taken place? At the present time, it is safe to say that the answer is unknown. More is constantly being learned about the operation of the brain, and there are many speculations about relationships between brain functioning and learning. However, any comprehensive or compelling description has yet to be developed.

ADDITIONAL ASPECTS
OF LEARNING

8

Early learning theories seemed to find it necessary to make explicit asumptions concerning neural connections, as in conditioned reflex units and in Thorndike's postulation of some sort of connection in the nervous system between stimulus and response. Field theorists make more general assumptions about the operation of the brain. Theorists like Skinner find it more fruitful not to speculate on brain processes, but to treat stimuli and responses operationally in terms of observable behavior; they are content to leave the brain process as a "black box."

It is obvious today that the conception of brain connections as a kind of telephone switchboard is entirely too simple. Certain areas of the brain have been mapped as governing certain specific functions. The maps of some sensory areas and motor areas are familiar to any student of human physiology. But this is less than half of the story. Specific functions for the brain are more unknown than known. There are apparently many rich interconnections among the some nine billion brain cells. The brain is active in the sense that there is constantly a pattern of nerve excitation or the firing of brain cells as electrochemical discharge. Studies of brain wave activity indicate that the brain is never entirely at rest. The picture of the passive organism waiting to be stimulated does not accord with our existing understanding of neural activity.

Studies of stimulus deprivation in which persons have been deliberately placed in situations where the usual external stimulation to touch, vision, hearing, and other sense modalities were eliminated as much as possible have reported bizarre mental activity. All sorts of hallucinations, delusions, and fantastic ideation occurred. Apparently, the brain cannot remain inactive.

Studies of brain damage and brain extirpation indicate that, to some extent, the function of specific known areas can be taken over by other areas not normally so used.

Some theorists have been impressed by the development of electronic computers (mechanical brains) as a kind of analogy for conceptualizing the working of the human brain. By this analogy, there must be facilitating circuits, inhibiting circuits, feedback circuits, and memory or storage circuits. This approach has some advantage in stimulating hypotheses and in permitting some vision of the complexities of brain functioning.

It is certainly true that we remember things in a variety of ways from habitual stereotyped behavior to quite distorted recollection of earlier experiences. Some of our memories trigger highly emotional reactions. Others are clear pictures without observable emotional response. How are these organized in the brain and either kept intact or distorted? There is some evidence, and more speculation, on the presence of reverberating circuits in the brain that keep memories alive. Their clarity or distortion probably depends upon the kind and number of interconnections between such circuits and other neural areas.

The fundamental process of perception was once explained in psychology by the mechanistic study of receptor organs and afferent neural transmission. Complex patterns were "obviously" a summing up of individual stimulations. This notion is not at all obvious today, and the neurological explanation of perception and its organization is recognized as an exceedingly complex interactive process.

To summarize this brief discussion, an understanding of the physiology of brain functioning must eventually be achieved in order to have a completely satisfying theory of learning. The brain is much more active and complex than earlier theories would imply. Perception and memory are fundamental to learning theory and need continued exploration at the physiological level. Those interested in understanding learning must remain aware of developments in this area.

SOME GENERAL CONCLUSIONS ABOUT LEARNING

As a conclusion to the discussion of learning *per se* (although there will be much discussion of learning in Part Three on development), some general conclusions may be proposed. In this presentation, aspects of learning theory and empirical studies that give us more concrete evidences about learning will be presented together. Some of the evidence has grown directly out of testing of the theories; other segments have been developed from practical or theoretical problems, not tied to any particular theory (35).

There has been a continuing tradition in American educational psychology for empirical investigations to be carried on independent of a defined systematic theory. Frequently, such studies originate in concerns of parents, teachers, or observers of learning situations who want to find out how or why particular things happen. In such cases, they may exist outside the mainstream of specific theories; and they may or may not eventually give support to such theories.

MATURATION AND READINESS

There is no denial in any of the theories that an individual learner must be able to respond to the learning situation and must be capable of giving the desired response before a particular learning can take place. Although a chimpanzee can be taught to articulate a few words, this is done with difficulty and never attains the characteristics that, in humans, we would call "learning to speak" (8). The physiological and psychological structure of the organism seems to preclude readiness for true speech. Some aspects of learning that are available to a ten-year-old child are not possible for a five-year-old. Readiness is partly built by biological differences in the growing organism and partly by learnings preliminary to the one under consideration.

In simple motor skills, empirical evidence clearly indicates that attempts to learn prior to normal physical maturation are at best inefficient and at worst inhibiting to further learning (6, 35). In more complex learnings, there is some evidence that the reorganization of preliminary learnings into a sequence and a time schedule different from the conventional pattern may affect readiness for the learning under consideration.

To put the statement more simply, we can learn to be "ready" in different ways; particular preliminary experiences will develop different patterns of readiness, given basic biological maturation.

An example of this concept is the recent interest in teaching very young children to read. According to conventional patterns it has generally been agreed that the child does not have readiness for "formal" instruction in reading until he has reached a mental age of six or six and a half. A variety of investigations with unusual preliminary experiences and unusual ways of organizing learning situations for reading indicate that children may be able to learn to read as early as at age three or four.

Because learning has long-range effects and because many specific learnings go into learning to read, there is no implication here that early reading is or is not desirable. The fact remains that a restructuring of preliminary learnings may redefine readiness for a particular complex learning. Careful definition of all learnings and their implications for future learning would be necessary to assess the desirability or danger of forcing readiness for a particular learning.

The frequent prescription for teaching stating that one must "start where the learner is" is derived from the readiness principle in learning. Indeed, the learner can start nowhere else than from "where he is." The particular learning that does take place will be partly a function of where he starts or the condition that he is in when he enters a particular learning situation. Actual learning may be quite different from desired learning because of the learner's particular conditions of readiness. It may be necessary for the individual to change his preliminary behavior, to "unlearn," before he can effectively engage in new learning situations.

MOTIVATION

In empirical investigations and in all theories discussed, there is some aspect of the learning process that can be called "motivation." Motivation is that which impels one to move, whether such impulsion is conscious or unconscious. It is not clear whether specific motivation is more fundamental to the process of learning or to demonstrating behavior that is the outcome of learning. In other words, does one *learn* better under particular conditions of motivations or does one simply *perform* learned acts better? Although this question is important to theory, it may have less practical significance because learning takes place through doing.

Motivation as a process may be thought of as both the internal or personal condition and the external situation to which one responds. The first aspect may be designated as motive and the second as incentive.

Some phase of needs theory must be invoked as the basic personal condition for motivation. Incentives that satisfy needs or are perceived as satisfying needs will be most potent in directing learning and behavior. Thus, intrinsic motivation, where needs are directly satisfied by the learning itself, is most efficient and probably produces the most efficient, pervasive, and permanent learning. Extrinsic motivation, in which secondary or intermediary incentives are used to carry the learning, is frequently necessary, but not as effective as the primary type.

Most of the empirical investigations have dealt with various extrinsic motivations. A great majority of these have been concerned with aspects of reward and punishment. Findings are remarkably consistent in indicating that the incentives defined as reward are more facilitative of learning than are punishments.

This is so logical and reasonable that it is surprising how slow teaching practices are to reflect it. Whether one sees the reward as acting directly upon the learning or as a mediating cue to the learning, it has become clear that rewarding a correct response (or a desired response) permits satisfaction to adhere to that response and makes it more likely to occur again under similar conditions. On the other hand, punishment may inhibit a particular response but gives no cue to the correct or desired one. Continued punishment continues to give no cue and fails to permit the adherence of satisfaction to any given response. In a sense, reward is self-enhancing, punishment is self-defeating.

However, few of the investigations have been able to demonstrate a one hundred percent efficacy for the defined reward or an absolute negative for the defined punishment. This is to be expected when we consider that, for the learner, reward and punishment are defined subjectively according to one's own motivational system. What the investigator plans as reward may not be so perceived by the learner.

This notion is well illustrated by demonstration of a special case of reward and punishment—praise and reproof or praise and blame—as an incentive to learning. In general, it has been true that, in classroom-learning situations, praise has played a more positive role than reproof. Praise is at least mildly rewarding, reproof mildly punishing. But this is not a "pure" variable. Accurate knowledge of results also tends to have positive motivational value in guiding learning activities. Praise and reproof, carrying implications of evaluative judgments of right and wrong, serve partly as such guidance. If the objective correctness is violated, so that praise and reproof are not related to actual performance, as in some experiments, the accurate knowledge of results can be eliminated as a motivator; however, the pupil's perception of the fairness or unfairness of the criticism is likely to cloud the situation.

Also, in general, obtaining the attention of the teacher is probably more rewarding for most pupils although not for all, than lack of attention. In this sense, being reproved may have more reward value than being ignored.

Keeping these complications in mind, a number of varied studies have confirmed that attention—whether praise or reproof—results in greater work output than lack of attention; that praise, as such, is slightly more motivating than reproof; that for children defined as introverted or for those with a school history of failure, praise is positive and reproof negative in effect; and that for children defined as extroverted or for those with a consistent school history of success, reproof tends to be more effective and praise less effective (35). Considered in the light of theoretical positions, these findings tend to support the theories that emphasize the importance of self-concept and the "optimistic" needs theories. Con-

82

sidered practically, they emphasize the importance of considering individual motivation and the differential effects of incentives. Finally, these investigations speak directly only about performance and productive output. Only by inference can they talk about "learning" *per se*.

A phenomenon that may be considered another special case of reward is perceived as dealing with learning as learning. Reinforcement as described in Skinnerian theory may be seen as a special kind of "reward," which, coming after a particular unit of behavior, tends to fix that behavior. This may not be motivation in the goal-directed sense, but it is akin to motivation in that the receiving of the reinforcement appears to satisfy an existing need or a general motivation in such a way that the aftereffect confirms the immediately prior behavior.

There has been enough checking on children of the reinforcement hypotheses, originally derived from laboratory animals, to be fairly certain that the general principles are applicable to at least some kinds of human learning, especially habitual sets and motor responses. In applied form, the principles may have to be extended and generalized beyond their original form.

In this context, reinforcement is not used in the customary manner of everyday discourse. Commonly, the term "reinforcement" is used to connote a summing up, a further confirmation of something already known. In this common sense, a reinforcement makes something stronger or increases the strength of an existing structure. If I "reinforce" something that you believe, I provide additional data or emotional support as a further test that confirms the position. In the special use of learning theory, reinforcement is the supplying of a condition after a specific behavior that tends to fix that behavior. When a rat receives a food pellet or a pigeon receives grain immediately after pressing a lever or pecking a delivery disk, it has received "reinforcement," which tends to fix the pressing or pecking behavior. The distinction may seem to be minor, but too often the two different usages have confused or blurred a clear understanding.

83

The special conditions of reinforcement are among the more interesting results of animal experimentation that can be applied to human learning. A basic principle is that reinforcement must be immediate. The rat or the pigeon must receive the food pellet or the grain immediately; the human learner must be praised, informed of the correctness of a response, or otherwise rewarded immediately after the response or the desired behavior. This principle has been applied most readily in the development of teaching machines or programmed learning, where the correct response is revealed immediately after the learner makes his response. It is equally applicable to tutorial situations. It is less commonly recognized that the same principle can be applied to organized work in small groups, where the interaction among a small group of learners working together provides the opportunity for mutual reinforcement.

Must reinforcement occur every time? Studies of reinforcement and extinction say no. Extinction is said to occur when the learned behavior

ceases. Its opposite is maintenance of the response or some degree of permanence in the learning. It has been well demonstrated that 100 per cent reinforcement (after each repetition of a correct response) leads to rapid extinction if the reinforcement is withdrawn. If, on the other hand, reinforcement occurs often enough to establish the response, but does not occur every time, the response is remarkably permanent or resists extinction for a considerable time, even without continuing reinforcement. Proper timing of immediate and intermittent reinforcements can establish behaviors that resist extinction. Thus, a child who has learned good study habits, arithmetic skills, or social studies information under proper conditions of reinforcement will be able to maintain these learnings with only occasional reinforcement. If, on the other hand, he has learned these things with the expectation of immediate reward every time he responds, withdrawal of reward will extinguish them (12, 25).

TENSION AND ANXIETY IN THE MOTIVATIONAL SYSTEM

Anxiety, a concept related to both personality and the external arrangement of conditions for learning, is receiving increased attention in psychological investigations. At one time it was assumed, primarily from the point of view of mental health, that anxiety was undesirable, and that the appropriate psychological aim was its reduction. With the recognition of the necessity of some kind of tension as an impulsion to learning activity, the positive effects of anxiety as a form of tension are beginning to be considered.

84

Studies of anxiety are, at this stage, extremely complex and varied (23, pp. 460-516). Generalizations must be tentative, but the direction of research findings seems to focus on the degree or intensity of anxiety as having differential effects. Because there is no clear-cut definition of "excessive" anxiety or of "some" anxiety, this discussion depends upon the reader's common-sense definitions.

Some anxiety, at a level where it may be reduced or made nonthreatening by a learning adaptation, appears to facilitate learning. At this level, anxiety serves as a drive—as a positive motivator—which, by its attention-focussing properties, directs learning activities and fixes their results by its drive reduction possibilities.

Excessive anxiety, at a level where it is too great to be reduced or made nonthreatening by a learning adaptation, has quite different effects. In directing attention, it will focus perception too narrowly on the anxiety-producing situation to permit a vision of possible solutions. A kind of "tunnel vision" exists, in which the necessary side pathways cannot be explored. The anxiety is interposed between the person and any objective consideration of the situation. The college student who is terribly anxious about academic failure keeps focussing on the possible results of failure, the impossibility of succeeding, the debilitating tension, and is unable to plan and engage in activities that would be objectively calculated to bring success.

Some degree of stress, tension, and anxiety facilitate learning. Too little brings complacency and lack of effort. Too much is seriously debilitating.

Research and theory have not yet defined these levels adequately in regard to motivation and learning.

In everyday school practice, much activity centers around assumptions concerning the motivational value of competition. It is commonly assumed that giving grades or marks as symbols of achievement on a competitive scale motivates pupils in a way consistent with the teacher's values. There has been remarkably little empirical investigation of these assumptions.

What evidence we do have in this area is perhaps better subsumed under what has already been said about self-concept, praise and reproof, and extrinsic motivation. Competition against oneself, the attempt to improve, is a strong motivation for those whose self-concept is expressed in a high level of aspiration. Competition against others is strong motivation only for those whose self-concept and need structure demand such evidence of status and esteem. For others, the competitive symbols are perceived as evidence of or references for knowledge of results in their work. Still others see these symbols not as competitive, but as evidence of the teacher's regard or praise, or as strictly secondary satisfiers having little direct relationship to the learning itself. In short, we have little evidence that the conventional focus on academic competition has any positive motivational value for learning. One may still wish to engage in competitive practices for other values, but the motivational values for learning have not been adequately demonstrated.

Cooperative structures, on the other hand, have received considerable attention, especially in social psychology. During those developmental periods in which relationships with peers are particularly important, cooperative contributions to the group and the carrying out of socially assigned roles have strong motivational values. There is considerable evidence that the acceptance of group-derived tasks and standards is a potent force in changing behavior in both school-age and adult groups.

It may be rather obvious but worthwhile to point out briefly the motivations likely to be operating in everyday learning situations. Without getting involved in detailed analyses, it should be apparent that such things as curiosity, task involvement, and the need for sheer physical activity when rested or for rest when tired are all common kinds of motivation to action and learning. Under certain conditions, the tendency to continue an activity once started and the tendency to engage in varied activity after an inactive period are sources for pacing and channeling learning activities. Prevailing interests and attitudes impel us to get involved in some things and not in others.

Tendencies to solve a problem or a puzzle, to complete a project that is under way, to "climb a mountain because it is there," appear to be relatively common motivations in man and the higher primates. The strength of such motivations probably depends upon the individual's self-concept and might be analyzed under concepts of needs structure. Practically, they cannot be ignored.

Most systematic learning theories treat motivation in a rather specific and narrow sense. That which the experimenter names as motivation and that which he focusses on as learning are the aspects that are dealt with. By experimental necessity, other possible motivations and other possible learnings tend to be ignored. In a broader sense, any living being, especially any human, is at all times motivated in some way to do something. The naturalistic assessment of learning must ask what learnings are going on under what conditions of motivation. For, surely, the person is learning something according to his current motivational system.

TRANSFER AMONG LEARNING EPISODES

One of the traditional topics in learning theory and in empirical studies of learning has been the question of the effects of learning in one situation on subsequent situations (35, pp. 187-218). The provision of schools for purposes of learning can only be justified on the assumption that what is learned will have some influence on the pupils' later everyday life. It is by no means obvious that this assumption is true or that the learnings anticipated in the school curriculum actually transfer to improved behavior in out-of-school situations.

If the general point of view about learning presented in Chapter 4 is accepted, transfer is inevitable. If we define learning outcomes as changes in the person demonstrable in overt behavior, subsequent situations will include those changes. The meaningful question then becomes, What kind of changes are related to what kind of subsequent effects?

If transfer takes place, it may be either positive or negative. Positive transfer facilitates subsequent learning or performance as, for example, learning to bat in a softball game effects improvement in driving a golf ball, or studying French makes easier certain aspects of learning Spanish. Negative transfer inhibits or gets in the way of subsequent performance as when one learns a specific procedure for handling a type of arithmetic problem and is, thereby, steered away from alternative procedures, which would be more effective in another problem. In other situations, there may be no transfer when the two sets of learnings are parts of different independent systems. A rather surprising example of the latter situation violates a very common-sense assumption in the teaching of English. It is generally assumed that the learning of formal grammar will transfer to improved writing and speaking. This is the usual reason given for teaching it. A number of studies show that there is very little transfer; knowing formal grammar has little observable effect on English usage and, certainly, has no automatic effect. This is not to say that positive transfer is not possible; however, it does point out that as grammar is usually taught and learned, transfer does not usually take place.

Apparently, learning somehow gets organized in systems with some sort of "boundary" between the systems. When two learnings are part of the same system, are learned as part of the same system, or are perceived as part of the same system, they may affect each other. For some children, in-school learnings form systems separate from out-of-school activities. For others, boundary lines cut across these categories and are organized so that greater transfer is possible. According to this analysis, the expressive activities of writing and speaking are part of a functional system that is separated from the intellectual and analytical activities of understanding the formal structure of the English language. For transfer to occur, these two systems must be brought together or created as a single system in the teaching-learning process. It is possible that current systems of functional grammar or structural linguistics may improve the possibilities of a system structured for effective transfer.

The classic example of problems of transfer may be analyzed in the same way. It was long thought that the study of Latin was particularly efficacious for general transfer value. Early studies of transfer failed to demonstrate this either in terms of general improvement in learning or in specific improvement in English. However, when the study of Latin was reorganized to focus on relationships between Latin and English to point up cognate forms and derivations, increasing transfer was demonstrated. A bridge had been built between the two systems.

It is commonly agreed that there are a number of ways of structuring learning to facilitate transfer:

1. Through identical elements. These may be identical in terms of facts or information, skills, methods, or principles of organization.
2. Through principles or generalizations from one learning situation or organized system that apply to other situations.
3. Through conscious efforts to perceive relationships and make applications of any learning.
4. Through developing an active intention to transfer or an attention to transferable phases.
5. Through greater stress on divergent thinking, open systems, or creative thinking that enhances transferability or decreases the rigidity of boundaries.

The last three statements are probably related to intelligence in the sense that these processes are more possible to the more highly intelligent. It is also possible that, to some extent, they can be learned. Some writers have stressed "learning to learn" or "learning how to learn" as a general mode of behavior that facilitates positive transfer. The above five approaches may be considered as involved in such a mode. For effective functioning, it is fundamental that we learn how to learn in ways that facilitate transfer.

Other implications of empirical investigations and theoretical applications might be discussed. The areas of readiness, motivation, and transfer have been considered as significant and illustrative of the learning process in action. For those interested in extending these illustrations or discovering their detailed sources, the bibliography appended to Part Two should be helpful.

1. ASSOCIATION FOR SUPERVISION AND CURRICULUM DEVELOPMENT, *Perceiving, Behaving, Becoming: A New Focus for Education*, 1962 Yearbook of the Association. Washington, D.C.: National Education Association, 1962.

2. BIGGE, MORRIS L. AND MAURICE P. HUNT, *Psychological Foundations of Education*. New York: Harper & Row, Publishers, 1962. A recent text with a point of view similar to that in this volume, but with a more detailed and extended treatment. Contains much discussion and many references that support the discussion in Chapter 8.

3. BRILL, A. A., tr. and ed., *The Basic Writings of Sigmund Freud*. New York: Modern Library, Inc., Random House, 1938.

4. COMBS, ARTHUR W. AND DONALD SNYGG, *Individual Behavior, A Perceptual Approach to Behavior*, rev. ed. New York: Harper & Row, Publishers, 1959.

5. FREUD, SIGMUND, *The Origins of Psycho-Analysis, Letters to Wilhelm Fliess, Drafts and Notes 1887-1902*. New York: Basic Books, Inc., 1954. The long story of the slow development of Freudian concepts is given reality in this series of letters and papers, written by Freud before and at the turn of the century.

6. GESELL, ARNOLD AND HELEN THOMPSON, "Twins T and C from Infancy to Adolescence: A Biogenetic Study of Individual Differences by the Method of Co-Twin Control," *Genetic Psychology Monographs*, XXIV (1941), 3-121. (Also appears in abridged form in Kuhlen and Thompson, cited below.) A report typical of studies that show the effects of readiness on motor-skill learning.

7. GUTHRIE, E. R., *The Psychology of Learning*. New York: Harper & Row, Publishers, 1952.

8. HAYES, KEITH J. AND CATHERINE HAYES, "The Intellectual Development of a Home-raised Chimpanzee," *Proceedings of the American Philosophical Society*, XCV (1951), 105-9. (Also appears in abridged form in Kuhlen, R. G. and G. G. Thompson, *Psychological Studies of Human Development*. New York: Appleton-Century-Crofts, 1952.)

9. HEIDBREDER, EDNA, *Seven Psychologies*. New York: Appleton-Century-Crofts, 1933. A classic treatment of varied theories and points of view in psychology.

10. HEBB, D. O., *The Organization of Behavior, A Neuropsychological Theory*. New York: Science Editions, Inc., 1961.

11. HILGARD, ERNEST, *Theories of Learning*, second ed. New York: Appleton-Century-Crofts, 1956. An extremely useful volume outlining and analyzing the major theories. Rather difficult reading for the beginning psychology student, but worthy of reference for those interested.

12. HOLLAND, JAMES G. AND B. F. SKINNER, *The Analysis of Behavior*. New York: McGraw-Hill Book Company, 1961. A text in the form of a linear program. Interesting both in point of view and as an illustration of principles of programmed learning.

13. HULL, C. L., *Essentials of Behavior*. New Haven, Conn.: Yale University Press, 1951.

14. KOFFKA, K., *The Growth of the Mind*. New York: Harcourt, Brace & World, Inc., 1924.

15. ———, *Principles of Gestalt Psychology*. New York: Harcourt, Brace & World, Inc., 1935.

16. KÖHLER, WOLFGANG, *Gestalt Psychology*. New York: Liveright Publishing Corp., 1947. (Also available as a paperback Mentor Book, 1959.)

17. ———, *The Mentality of Apes*. New York: Harcourt, Brace & World, Inc., 1925.

18. LEWIN, K., *A Dynamic Theory of Personality*. New York: McGraw-Hill Book Company, 1935.

19. ———, *Principles of Topological Psychology*. New York: McGraw-Hill Book Company, 1936.

20. MASLOW, ABRAHAM H., *Motivation and Personality*. New York: Harper & Row, Publishers, 1954.

21. MURRAY, HENRY A., *Explorations in Personality*. New York: Oxford University Press, Inc., 1938.

22. NATIONAL SOCIETY FOR THE STUDY OF EDUCATION, *The Psychology of Learning*, Forty-first Yearbook, Part II. Chicago: University of Chicago Press, 1942. An exposition of the several systems of learning theory by exponents of each point of view. Places somewhat greater stress on implications for teaching than do the references oriented strictly toward psychology.

23. ———, *Child Psychology*, Sixty-second Yearbook, Part I. Chicago: University of Chicago Press, 1963. Something of a new departure in works on child psychology in that it concentrates on research on such variables as anxiety, achievement, aggression, and dependence more than on the more usual developmental topics.

24. ROGERS, CARL R., *Counseling and Psychotherapy*. Boston: Houghton Mifflin Company, 1942.

25. SKINNER, B. F., *Science and Human Behavior*. New York: The Macmillan Company, 1953.

26. ———, *Walden Two*. New York: The Macmillan Company, 1948. A contemporary utopia indicating Skinner's perception of a sub society, organized according to scientific principles.

27. THOMPSON, CLARA, *Psychoanalysis: Evolution and Development*. New York: Hermitage House, 1950. A description and analysis not only of classical Freudian theory and early deviations, but also of more recent developments by such theorists as Horney, Fromm, and Sullivan.

28. THORNDIKE, E. L., *Animal Intelligence: Experimental Studies*. New York: The Macmillan Company, 1911. Students interested in a direct reading of Thorndike, in order to get the flavor of his point of view, will find this and the following three references most helpful.

29. ———, *The Fundamentals of Learning*. New York: Teachers College, Columbia University Press, 1932.

30. ———, *The Psychology of Learning, Educational Psychology*, Vol. II. New York: Teachers College, Columbia University Press, 1913.

31. ———, *The Psychology of Wants, Interests, and Attitudes*. New York: Appleton-Century-Crofts, 1935.

32. THORPE, LOUIS P. AND ALLEN M. SCHMULLER, *Contemporary Theories of Learning*. New York: The Ronald Press Company, 1954. A series of interpretations of theories of learning. Pays more attention to philosophical bases and implications than does Hilgard.

33. TOLMAN, E. C., *Behavior and Psychological Man.* Berkeley and Los Angeles, Calif.: University of California Press, 1958. Includes many of Tolman's papers over the years 1922-1948. Especially important for the interpretation of Tolman in this volume are the articles appearing on pp. 144-178 and 241-264.

34. ——, *Purposive Behavior in Animals and Men.* Berkeley and Los Angeles, Calif.: University of California Press, 1949.

35. TRAVERS, ROBERT M. W., *Essentials of Learning.* New York: The Macmillan Company, 1963. An excellent summary and interpretation of research on learning. Especially good on neuro-physiological areas and conclusions from empirical studies. Goes into much greater depth on material dealt with in Chapter 8 of this volume. An excellent bibliography, which will refer students to many of the problems and findings discussed.

36. WALTER, W. GREY, *The Living Brain.* New York: W. W. Norton & Company, Inc., 1953.

37. WATSON, JOHN B., *Psychological Care of Infant and Child.* New York: W. W. Norton & Company, Inc., 1928.

38. ——, *Psychology from the Standpoint of a Behaviorist.* Philadelphia: J. B. Lippincott Co., 1919.

PART THREE THE NATURE AND
DEVELOPMENT OF THE LEARNER

In Parts One and Two of this volume, an attempt has been made to analyze certain aspects of the teaching and learning process that may be helpful to the prospective teacher or may be of interest to those concerned with education in American schools today.

It is equally necessary to look at some discoveries concerning the person who does the learning. Each of us has a life history. Certain aspects of that life history are held in common with all life histories. Others are common to life histories in a particular culture. Still others are unique to the individual. Part Three will attempt to sort out some of the factors and principles that apply to these phases of the development of the individual learner. Biologically, the human being has a longer period of dependency than any other known being. Increasingly, in modern civilization, this dependency is culturally extended even longer than is biologically necessary. These two facts have tremendous significance for human behavior in general and for individual behavior of human beings. Individual behavior is a result of the interaction between the relatively slow biological development of the human being and the particular physical and social

THE DEVELOPMENTAL POINT OF VIEW

9

forces playing upon that development. Being dependent for a long time, the human being is more plastic, more subject to the molding of his environment, than most other species. The variations of possible environmental influences provide more opportunity for individual differences in humans than in species that mature over a shorter period of time.

For the prospective teacher, it may be useful to understand as much as possible about both the common characteristics and the unique qualities of the organisms he will teach. It is tempting for the high school teacher to try to limit his study to behavior during the adolescent years. It is equally tempting for the elementary teacher to feel that he need not know what happens developmentally after his time of contact with children. Developmental theory insists that a working understanding at any level depends upon some understanding of past, present, and potential future. A particular twelve-year-old acts the way he does partly because of things that have happened to him over the past twelve years, partly because of things that are happening to him now, and partly because of expectations and possibilities yet to come. Some of these happenings are typical of most twelve-year-olds, some are unique to the particular individual. As we look at the nature and development of the learner, it will be our task to understand regular expected events and to look at some significant probabilities for individual differences.

COMMON HEREDITY AND INDIVIDUAL HEREDITY

The life of individual human beings starts with the union of a male and female reproductive cell, a sperm and an ovum. It is commonly recognized that this union makes possible a unique human being, necessarily different from any other human being. Thus, we each represent a unique biological heredity, never, as far as we know, duplicated.

The closest approach to duplication occurs in identical twins or other multiples of identity when the initial fertilized cell splits into two or more separate organisms. Even here, with a common genetic constitution, there are still biological differences. One common difference lies in the fact that twins may show reversed laterality or opposite brain dominance. Thus, one twin may become right-handed, the other left-handed. Genotypical likeness does not preclude phenotypical differences. The hereditary mechanism works in a way that assures individual differences.

On the other hand, genetic inheritance also assures likenesses. All offspring of human beings are identifiable as members of the species Homo sapiens. They have common characteristics, which lie within an identifiable range. The great majority of human beings fall within a very narrow range of difference, in regard to any particular characteristic. The hereditary likenesses within mankind are greater than the individual differences. These biological characteristics of human beings provide the basis whereby we can think about individual differences. A rat is a rat, a dog is a dog, and a man is a man. The three have characteristics that enable us to classify them as mammals, and their offspring will run true to form. We can predict general characteristics of behavior that will be common to the general classifications. This is the underlying principle of heredity, which permits meaningful study of the behavior of human beings and enables us to promulgate descriptions of human behavior as such. It is this principle that makes it possible to recognize likenesses and explain differences.

Having considered the homogeneity and relatively narrow range of differences of mankind, we must quickly return to the tremendous variety of possible combinations of characteristics available to an individual. The blueprint for individual development is provided by the nature of the cellular material—known as chromosomes—which, in some way not completely known, determines the course of biological development and physiological functioning. Each of the billions of cells comprising an individual's body carries the same unique trademark, a distinctive pattern of chromosomes shared by no other body.

It is important to note that, strictly speaking, the only characteristic inherited is the cellular blueprint for physical structure. Practically then, with some modifications by environment, physical structures are inherited. Only to the extent that physical structure determines functioning is behavior inherited. A child cannot inherit his father's disposition. He can inherit the determiners of a particular set of physical structures that operate in certain ways, including his typical energy output and his capabilities of perceiving the world around him. It is out of this physical structure, capable of functioning in varied ways, that the psychological person develops.

PRENATAL DEVELOPMENT

As far as we know, the period from conception to birth is one of physical growth—in size, weight, and differentiation. In spite of old wives' tales, there is little evidence to support notions of *psychological* influences on the organism in utero. There are, however, physical or biological influences that affect the course of development. Children born with noticeable abnormalities may exhibit these as a result of hereditary (genetic) characteristics or as a result of intra-uterine influences, birth damage, or from a combination of these factors. Except for certain specific carefully studied anomalies, the fixing of specific cause is extremely difficult.

The development of the organism in utero is influenced by (1) the genetic pattern set at conception, including species characteristics and individual characteristics; (2) the condition of nourishment and oxygen supply, including gross and subtle chemical, vitamin, and toxic conditions; and (3) the condition of physical protection or damage. By birth, the infant has already been affected by many physical and biochemical events and is already well started on an individual life history.

The interaction of these conditions gives an excellent illustration of one of the major themes of development, the juxtaposition of critical developmental stages with particular environmental events.

There has been much confusion on the relative influence of "heredity" and "environment," frequently put in the form of a question, "Which is more important . . . ?"

The position taken here and serving as one of the guidelines in our look at the development and behavior of the learner is that this is essentially a meaningless question. Without a biological heredity, there would be no organism for environment to act upon. Without environmental support, there would be no continuation of the biological organism. The meaningful question is, "How do environmental events and the biological organism interact to produce what results?"

It seems clear that one important element in answering this question is that of the juxtaposition of a particular environmental event with a particular stage of development. No two children in the same family can experience precisely the same psychological environment because a simultaneous event that occurs in a family occurs at different developmental times for different siblings. Teachers need to be aware of this juxtaposition, since the introduction of particular information cannot interact with a nine-year-old child in the same way that it would with a seven-year-old.

At birth, the infant can be recognized as an individual. There is continuity between what he has been, what he is, and what he will be. He has certain observable characteristics, and he tends to behave in ways that help to identify his uniqueness. We refer to these surface characteristics and to manifest behavior as *phenotypical*. That is, they define the infant in an observable way. Underlying these are the *genotypical* characteristics, those underlying genetic determinants that set some phases of his development—his present and future behavior—even though there is no visible evidence of them. Although growth, development, and learning are based upon the genotype, we can describe and assess them only in terms of phenotypical change.

READINESS

It will be apparent that another theme is now implicit in our discussion. It is evident that optimum development requires an appropriate environment when the blueprint is ready for the next stage. It is equally evident that the organism must be at an appropriate stage of development before it can use the nurturing environment. This theme of readiness for utilizing external events will become even more important as we move into the next stage of psychological development.

In order to look at the development of the newborn child into a unique adult, two conceptual schemes will be used to organize the discussion. The first is a modified version of the Freudian concepts of psychosexual stages of development. The second is the notion of developmental tasks. Both conceptualizations accept the assumptions we have already made concerning readiness and the importance of the interaction of a given organism with environmental events.

PSYCHOSEXUAL STAGES

The neonate, a going organism with certain growth trends, is only potentially a person. His capabilities for growth and reaction are dependent upon the support of others. The ways in which this support is given and denied and his reaction to this pattern of support determine the kind of person he will become. Obviously, some events are crucial in the first few days; others assume importance later. The birth process has profoundly changed the pattern of environmental support and stimulation. Even though the womb may have been increasingly unsatisfactory as a growth medium, it still

A BROAD VIEW OF PSYCHOLOGICAL DEVELOPMENT: INFANCY AND EARLY CHILDHOOD

10

provided continuous nourishment to the organism. Stability of temperature, satisfaction of oxygen needs, and relative reduction of sensory stimulation were all automatic. Relatively suddenly, all this changes. The organism is exposed to unusual pressures, to massive sensory stimulation, to the use of chest muscles in a new mode of receiving oxygen, to the rhythms of deprivation and satiation in new modes of receiving nutrients. He is almost as dependent as before, but without the automatic safeguards. Someone must intentionally provide for him. Some writers have contended that the infant appears to be in a state resembling "shock" for a period of time following the birth process. Certainly, the organism must make profound adjustments to a new environment.

THE ORAL PERIOD

The infant's mouth and oral reactions assume earliest importance as a focus for psychological development. His earliest needs are physiological and are best coped with by the mouth. The best developed and most active muscles of the neonate are those of the mouth. He was able to suck and swallow before birth. Breathing and eating are done through the mouth, and he literally starts to take in the world around him with his mouth. Apparently, there is something akin to pleasure in the stimulation of the mouth; as the rhythm of hunger and feeding develops, it is the mouth that is active prior to relief of hunger. The basic theme of psychological development, the alternation of frustration and satisfaction of needs, begins with feeding behavior in this period.

It appears that it takes a while for the infant to differentiate a perception of himself and others. This is, indeed, a long slow process of learning. Initially, he really has no "self"; he is simply an organism with physiological maintenance needs. When in need of nourishment, the bottle or breast that feeds him is a part of his organism as the placenta had been before. Psychologically, he is an energy system demanding satisfaction. Freudian theory characterizes this as domination by the "pleasure principle."

Satisfaction does not come on demand. There are periods of time when hunger is not satiated. The total system does not work right. To go beyond the oral activities, there are times when he is uncomfortable in other ways and is not comforted. Gradually, as maturation continues and as cortical organization makes possible better perception and motor activity, he begins to identify objects outside of himself and to differentiate his organism from others. He comes to identify the comforters and punishers in the world around him. By sixteen weeks, he appears to recognize his mother (or other providers of satisfaction). There seems to be some recognition of the fact that satisfactions and frustrations are provided by others. He learns that satisfactions are not spontaneous, that he cannot always have what he wants when he wants it. The "pleasure principle" starts to give way to the "reality principle" as he begins to adapt his behavior in terms of others and starts to develop his "self," his ego. He starts to "understand" the world in which he lives and begins to act in accordance with that understanding.

In both gross and subtle ways, the people around the infant have been providing critical information for the building of this ego-in-the-world. The provision or withholding of food so that frustration periods are short or long, differing degrees of sucking satisfaction provided by the mode of feeding, the emotional experiences of parents and the degree of security with which they hold the baby, the speed with which discomfort is allayed—all these and many other ways of patterning the frustration-satisfaction sequence are fundamental to the beginnings of psychological development.

The infant who is regularly fed before he is hungry lives in a very different world from the child who is forced to endure hunger for long periods of time. The child on "demand feeding" has a very different series of experiences from the one on a rigid predetermined schedule. The businesslike "no-nonsense" mother tells a very different story of the world to her child than the cuddling, protective mother. The mother who handled her first child anxiously and insecurely may provide very different information about the world to her second child.

During the first part of the oral period, the infant is almost totally dependent as he takes in food and information. His only expression or active control possibilities lie in another oral activity, crying. Here again, the way significant people respond to the crying provides some evidence of the amount of control and self-assertion the developing ego will have. Later, a more active assertive phase of oral behavior develops as the baby becomes able to bite, chew, and actively engage in eating solid food. The critical activity of this period is weaning, a real series of steps toward maturity. Since this activity is among the first major opportunities for self-control and assertion, refusals to eat or to "eat properly" are not uncommon. There are still so few ways to assert one's developing individuality. The climax of this period is the beginning of another oral activity, speech (1, 2, 8, 9, 27).

99

THE ANAL PERIOD

By the end of the first year, the developmental focus shifts from one end of the digestive tract to the other. The child's interests and pleasures are likely to show heightened concern with both the process and products of elimination. This period is referred to as the anal period and continues to about the end of the third year. In our culture, we strengthen the importance of this period by stressing toilet training, cleanliness training, modesty, and self-control.

To the child, the products of elimination are not initially perceived as "dirty," disgusting, or unacceptable. On the contrary, they have interesting properties of texture, color, odor, and variety. This attractiveness is enhanced by the discovery that they are products of his own body. They are something the child does or makes himself. Furthermore, the process of releasing them is pleasurable in itself and a relief of tension when completed. Apparently, early in the anal period, the child does not have the insight into body functions to recognize the relationship between his activity and his waste products. Physiologically, he does not have sufficient muscular development to control the expulsion of waste until about 18 months. Between the beginning and end of the anal period, much learning and self-control are developed with profound psychological results.

To understand this process, we must digress to another fundamental concept, ambivalence. In his emotional reactions to the frustrations and satisfactions of the oral period, the child has developed a response of like and dislike toward his parents. When they are satisfiers, his total reaction of comfort includes them and invests them with the qualities of loved objects. Equally, when they provide frustrations, his feelings of dissatisfaction encompass them in a reaction akin to hate. As the ego develops and the reality principle is applied, some identification processes start the child wanting to please and to become like the "good" parents. On the other hand, he may or may not want to be like the "bad" parents. This conflict takes a long time to resolve and provides a basic dynamic during both the anal and the next period. At the same time, it must be remembered that the parents are not entirely unambivalent about their child. They may or may not love him in the way romantic fiction would indicate. Certainly, at times he annoys them intensely. Love and hate are frequently close together on an emotional scale, not only for infants.

The crucial tasks of the oral period need not invoke the hate side of ambivalence to nearly the degree that the tasks of the anal period do. In general, the desires of both parents and child for appropriate feeding behavior and oral satisfaction tend to be congruent. Both the child's well-being and the parents' desires tend in the same direction if both are relatively healthy. This is not true of the anal period. In modern society, both reality and the parents' deeply ingrained training run counter to the child's desire for unfettered pleasure in defecation and urination. Even the most relaxed and permissive parents in a modern American home can scarcely be happy with the results of these childish pleasures. They want him to eliminate at what they consider the proper place and time.

The resolution of this potential conflict is handled by the process of substitute satisfactions inherent in the reality principle. If the child has weathered the oral period and achieved the appropriate level of maturity, he basically wants the approval of the "good" parents. He wants to do what pleases mother. His ego development also permits him to perceive that, *for about the first time,* he can do something on his own; he can exert some control over the world, he can give of himself. The products of his body are valuable to him, and they seem important to his mother. He can please her and assert himself by giving her these gifts at the appropriate time and place. As he moves from the expulsive phase of this period to the later retentive phase, he can also withhold his gifts. He also comes to have pleasure in physiological self-control and in the long-term rhythms of withholding and releasing.

It is during this period that some of the prohibitions and commands, wishes and desires, attitudes and feelings of the parents are impressed upon the child in ways that go beyond identification, to become introjection of parental values within the child's character structure. Some of the more painful aspects of the anal period are repressed, and superego functions are developed and internalized. Some aspects of the lessons learned contribute to ego development and become part of conscious values. Others become part of the superego, exerting control in a more pervasive way as part of the basic structure of the personality.

Many people find it difficult to accept this description of development during the anal stage. It must be admitted that there is little direct evidence to support it. Like much of the material on psychosexual stages, it rests on its plausibility and its power in providing a framework for explaining some aspects of personality development that would otherwise require even more bizarre explanations. Like much of psychoanalytical theory, it is best supported by protocols from therapy, which indicate that something went wrong in this process resulting in personality malfunction. Certainly, there is much that can go wrong in the complexities of resolving the conflicts inherent in this description. A number of personal characteristics are modified during the anal period. Basic behaviors of generosity and penury are said to be affected by reactions in this period. Even physiological functioning as in normal bowel control can be learned too well and result in the kind of withholding called "constipation." Attitudes toward dirt and cleanliness are developed here, so that compulsive neatness or extreme filth may result as enduring personal characteristics. Attitudes of acceptance or shame about normal body functions may be seen as having their origins in this period (1, 2, 8, 9, 27).

THE PHALLIC PERIOD

During the third year, attention to body function shifts from anal activity to an intensified interest in the genital organs. This continues as the focus of development until about the sixth year and results in the completion of the basic personality. Some writers refer to this as the genital period, but that term will be reserved here for a later more mature period of sexual interest. Rather, the term "phallic" is used, implying a more symbolic use of sexual material, as well as the concentration on sexual organs as such rather than as part of a functioning system.

Genotypical sex differentiation was set at conception. Phenotypical sex differentiation has been distinguishable since the third month after conception. One of the first questions asked at the birth of a child in our culture is, "Is it a boy or a girl?" From that moment on, parents and others structure the world to provide differential social-sexual identifications. There is probably some difference in the physical handling of boy babies and girl babies. Clothing, playthings, and transmitted parental expectations of behavior are all used to help the child identify his sex and behave in conformity with its cultural definition. This process reaches its peak during the phallic period, resulting in the internalization of sexual identification and the values and attitudes toward self and sexual activity.

As the child attempts to structure the world around him and his relationship to it, he engages in much fantasy as a way of making sense out of things that are beyond his realistic understanding. Probably, the most important aspects of the world to him in the early years are the interrelationships in his own family. As he becomes physically more autonomous, he explores his environment more independently; however, his curiosity outruns his ability to understand. It has long been noted that many ancient myths and legends from a variety of cultures have much in common with each other and with the fantasies of children. One of these myths is the story of Oepidus, selected by Freud and labelled the "Oedipus complex" (21), to serve as the analogy of the conflicts of the phallic period. In this brief description of the Oedipus story, a possible child's eye view is juxtaposed.

Laius and Jocasta, king and queen of Thebes ("Mother and father are powerful people"), are warned by an oracle ("People know what I am thinking") that their newborn son, Oedipus, will grow up to kill his father ("I will become more powerful than he; I wish he were dead") and marry his mother ("If he goes away I will take his place"). The king orders his infant son killed ("If he knows about this, he will try to kill me"), but the boy is not killed ("I will escape somehow"). He is raised by others ("I need someone to take care of me") as their son ("Are they really my parents?"). He returns and, not knowing the relationship, kills Laius, marries Jocasta, and becomes king. Upon discovering what he has done, he is overcome with guilt ("I would really feel sorry if he were dead"), puts out his own eyes ("I had better stop seeing some things"), and is later destroyed by the gods ("This is pretty dangerous stuff").

It is postulated that something of this sort actually goes on in the child's mind as he adjusts to the relationships within his family. He receives relatively less care and attention as he completes the process of toilet training. Father is a competitor for his mother's attention. Some children will verbally indicate the wish that their father go away, so that they can have mother to themselves. They will talk of marriage to mother. Yet, father is big and powerful and a dangerous competitor. Also, the attitude toward both father and mother is ambivalent.

The conflict is typically resolved by the boy's delaying his desire for the mother and identifying with his image of the father. ("I will be like father and will eventually grow up and marry someone like mother.") This involves internalizing a great many values, prohibitions, and commands relating to sexual activity. The fear of the conflict is too great to be kept alive, and the memories of the conflict need to be buried under threat of guilt feelings. Out of this, the structure of the superego becomes relatively complete. Many of the events of childhood are repressed and are not available to conscious memory.

The situation for the girl is somewhat different and perhaps more complex. She goes through a similar feeling of desire for the attention of father and competition with mother. She must resolve the conflict by identifying with the mother figure and orienting her eventual sexual activity toward a male figure like father.

For both boy and girl, the identifications accepted in this period set the stage for future sexual adjustments. Some theorists put much greater stress on "castration fear" and "penis envy" concepts, making central the recognition that the boy has a penis and the girl does not. In this version, the boy's fear of retaliation is of the actual loss of his penis. The girl's motivation is the desire for one. Certainly, some children have fantasies that include physical sexual behavior and physical retaliation. Some boys believe that girls were once little boys who were bad and have had their penises cut off.

Other theorists and the results of some recent research put much greater stress on the positive love relationship as dominant in this period. Identification is seen as resulting more from desire to be like the loving and loved parents than from fear and threat of punishment or harm. There are other alternative explanations of the dynamics of identification (15, pp. 107-51).

The events of the phallic period are indeed complex. Obviously, there are many possible variations on the theme of resolution of the conflict. Unhealthy attitudes toward sexual behavior, extreme prohibitions, improper sex identifications, and extreme fear and guilt feelings can be ascribed to the complexities of this period.

There is a great deal of magic in this period. The child who loses a parent by death, desertion, or unexplained absence after he has wished him dead or gone may feel responsible for his loss. The fears and guilt feelings associated with such an event can be most traumatic. The models provided by father and mother during this period are crucial to the kind of adult the child will become and the kind of adjustment he will make. Identification is never pure; the boy will incorporate some of the mother's image, the girl some of the father's. The image is as the child sees it rather than as it truly is. Thus, the child may see the parent as more dominant or punishing than he really is. He incorporates such values into his superego. Reaction formation may occur, so that the child uses something like a reverse image in his personality building. His reactions to teachers as he goes to school will depend partly on the kind of adjustment he has made to the adults in his family during this period.

Curiosity and the drive to find out may be built out of the prototypical reactions of this period. As the child finds out that it does or does not pay to investigate and ask questions, his potential reaction to the world of knowledge will be affected (1, 2, 8, 9, 21, 27).

DEVELOPMENTAL TASKS

Another way of looking at development involves the concept of the developmental task. Any society demands certain adjustments and behavior on the part of its members. People in any group are expected to feel, think, and act in certain ways. For some societies, possible variations in expected behavior are quite restrictive; in other societies, wide variations are possible. The process of learning to respond to these demands and of becoming the kind of person a particular society expects is known as "socialization."

Central to the preceding discussion has been the needs of the child and his changing readiness for new demands. There is some danger of thinking of this as a "natural" process rather than as a socially dictated one. Equally dangerous is the tendency of some theorists to deal only with external pressures and to ignore internal development. The socialization of the child and his development to maturity requires the complex interweaving of internal needs and external demands. The developmental task concept makes both sides of this process explicit.

At each stage of development, what does the child need to do to be ready to move on to the next stage? What is he ready to do that will make it possible for him to master the required tasks? In order to achieve relatively successful and happy maturity, what series of tasks are necessary in our society? Is there a sequence of tasks that fits the child's present readiness, the achievement of which makes it possible for him to move on to the next stage? These are the questions that are dealt with in the notion of developmental tasks. The description of the early stages is not unlike the preceding description of the oral, anal, and phallic stages. The discussion, however, does not depend upon an underlying theory of development; it may be derived from empirical observation of children in our culture. The details of the tasks vary in different societies, and the subtleties of how they are carried out make for wide variation in our own society.

There are a number of ways of describing the developmental tasks. The discussion here is based largely upon Havighurst's treatment in *Human Development and Education* (17).

DEVELOPMENTAL TASKS OF INFANCY AND EARLY CHILDHOOD

ACHIEVING PHYSIOLOGICAL STABILITY

This first task in point of time and logical sequence is the most purely biological of the tasks, but it depends on social care for its successful completion. The neonate is still physiologically unstable. The post-uterine rhythms must be established. Temperature regulation is still labile, easily varying widely during infancy and early childhood as compared to adult body temperature. The balancing of the various contents of the blood stream takes time. Probably, the only social influences affecting this task are subtle psychosomatic influences provided by the level of anxiety or security expressed by adults in handling the variable infant (17, p. 15; 17A, p. 12).

LEARNING TO TAKE SOLID FOODS

Discussion of the oral period has indicated the basic importance of this task for personality development. This is one of the first major tasks leading from dependence toward independence. From the point of view of socialization, all of the details of attitude toward food, food tabus, development of approved eating behavior, and the emotional climate surrounding eating are basic learnings associated with this central task. Basic trust or distrust of the world and others are enhanced in the provision of food and the rituals surrounding its use. The encouragement of passive or active eating behavior starts to form the pattern of passivity or aggressiveness in other behavior (17, p. 10; 17A, p. 7).

In some cultures, the break between breast feeding and the use of solid foods is sharp, sometimes early, and probably highly frustrating. In others, breast feeding is continued as long as the child wishes and no sharp distinction is made. Taking solid foods is accomplished without any concern for weaning. In our society, customs have changed over several generations. The current norm seems to be a rather early introduction of semisolid textured foods along with bottle feeding (more often than breast feeding), and the gradual reduction of the use of the bottle with some pressures toward more adult modes of eating.

Along with this comes the first introduction of the use of tools and implements, perhaps an important learning in our machine culture.

LEARNING TO TALK

Language development is so closely tied to concept formation and intellectual development in our culture that it carries a heavy load in the socialization process. Processes of symbolization and verbalization set the stage for a large part of future learning. There is some evidence that a child who fails to learn to speak by the beginning of the latency period will be almost irreversibly damaged in total development (17, p. 10; 17A, p. 7).

Speech itself is not an isolated behavior; it is the outward evidence of a whole verbal way of behavior (2). Meaningful speech is preceded by the recognition that sounds mean something. The infant makes noises with his speech mechanisms, first just because they are there and he is organized physiologically so that sounds are produced. Concurrently, he hears the speech sounds made by others. Somewhere along the way, he makes the discovery of the regularity of association of some sounds with some activities and things. Apparently, it takes some time to differentiate and discriminate precise details of the sounds. This does not stop him from trying them out himself and discovering again that other people respond to his sounds. Some children will put forth a long series of statements that sound like speech complete with inflection and expressive gestures. Yet, there is not a conventional word in the entire production. This seems to indicate that the child has differentiated a general pattern of speech, which he tries himself before he distinguishes words and their meanings. Other children may seem to be slow in using speech and then, relatively suddenly, begin speaking in quite clear phrases. These examples give evidence that there is a great deal of verbal learning before the child verbalizes aloud. Most children play with language a great deal with many false starts and successes. Clear, individual words combine with gibberish and sounds that are close to recognizable words.

In the first three years of life, the human child accomplishes a task that, as far as we know, no other known organism has ever accomplished —the basic mastery of speech and the use of it for communication and manipulation of ideas. In observations of chimpanzees and other primates, the inability to master speech seems to be the major difference between them and humans. Most other tasks demanded of the human infant are mastered by the chimpanzee more readily because of his more rapid rate of maturation. He responds to language, though probably the nonverbal expressive aspects are at least as important as the verbal. He may be taught, with difficulty, to enunciate several words and to associate them correctly. Beyond this he cannot go, and such learnings seem to be relatively temporary. Animals that impress us with their ability to learn to speak, such as parrots and some other birds, do not adopt a verbal way of behavior and do not seem to get the "idea" of language. As far as we know, the task of learning to talk is a uniquely human task.

By the end of the first year, the infant is responding socially to the language of others. His parents may recognize two or three "words" that he uses with apparent meaning. He vocalizes on social contact, but probably does not yet use expressive jargon. By a year and a half, a great deal of preverbal learning has gone on in preparation for speech. Expressive jargon is quite common, and about ten definite words can be identified (11, pp. 190-91).

Between eighteen months and two years, amazing things happen to language development. Jargon has given way to a speech pattern that may be identified as the "three-word-sentence" structure. The average American child at two has about 300 words in his vocabulary, although some children may have as many as a thousand and some only a few. The growth of vocabulary in this six-month period is quite remarkable. Language learning is very active, with much repetition and playing with phrases. By three, the average American child has a vocabulary of about 1,000 words and is speaking in real sentences with quite a high degree of sophistication. He is still in an active stage of learning to perfect his use of language. Accompanying dramatic play with a stream of verbalizations, he notes the reactions of others to his speech. His use of pronouns and verb tenses is well developed. From here on, speech development is a matter of expansion, refinement, and increasing application to abstractions. Basically, the average three-year-old has conquered this developmental task (11, pp. 191-204).

With developing language learning and its manifestation in speech, the child probably uses language as one way of handling the conflicts of the anal and phallic stages. He asks questions of others and probably asks questions of himself. He verbalizes the answers and manipulates words to give explanations to himself and to give himself directives and commands. He will organize his activity by announcing what he is doing and what he intends to do. He is now capable of saying, as well as feeling, "She doesn't love me," or "I hate you." By putting feelings into words, they can be handled differently. The sequence of events and causes are better controlled through language. The "if–then" pattern of thinking that was implicit in the partial renunciation of the pleasure principle can now be made explicit in the continued development of the reality principle. The refinement of the ego and superego would probably not be possible without the aid of language.

LEARNING TO WALK

Postural adaptations during the first few weeks of life are the beginnings of motor development that will eventuate in walking alone less than a year and a half later. Because of body proportions and slower growth rate of the extremities as compared to head and upper trunk, the child's walking behavior will continue to differ markedly from that of the adult for some time. Yet by eighteen months or two years, he is capable of independent locomotion in an upright position (11, pp. 70-75; 17, p. 9; 17A, p. 6).

Walking, as such, is largely dependent on maturation; it requires a minimum of practice and social stimulation. In cultures that confine the child to a cradle board, or in other ways restrict freedom of movement, walking takes place at approximately the same time as in ours. The socialization pressures that accompany learning to walk make this a significant developmental task. The tension between restriction and independence provides a kind of security and a definition of the world to be explored. The quality of the world and appropriate behavior in it are subtly differentiated by the different devices for restricting and channelling walking behavior. As walking permits new modes of exploration and places to explore, adult attitudes toward exploring and their provision of things to explore are varied from child to child.

It is possible that an achievement-oriented culture like contemporary America is maintained and strengthened by the encouragement and praise given to most children for evidence of achievement in walking. Coming at the same time as reward for achievement in toilet training, these two activities present possibilities for reward or punishment in the achievement area that may have great influence on the child and his developing self-concept. Walking a month earlier than most children of the same age is no true achievement; however, the typical family treats it as one in praising the child and bragging to the neighbors. More common is the expressed concern over the child who falls behind in walking behavior.

The task itself tends to be accomplished when the organism is physically ready. Its psychological importance comes in the social and emotional situation attached to it.

LEARNING TO CONTROL THE ELIMINATION OF BODY WASTES

This task has already been dealt with as the central feature of the anal period. Its formulation in the language of developmental tasks emphasizes the child's responsibilities in this function more than does the more passive term "toilet training." The child who has not accomplished this task by the time he enters school is a child in trouble. He is in social trouble because of society's demands. He is probably also in emotional trouble, which is demonstrated in the symptoms of control failure (17, p. 14; 17A, p. 11).

LEARNING SEX DIFFERENCES AND SEXUAL MODESTY

This is one of the central tasks to be accomplished during the phallic period. In addition to the basic sexual identifications and attitudes, differentiation of interests and behavior of boys and girls is also expected. The specific social behavior associated with sex differences will become more important during the next stage. However, by the end of early childhood, the boy is expected not only to feel like a boy, but to look and act like one. Little girls at this age are likely to have less pressure for conformity to allegedly feminine behavior, but there is greater acceptance of behavior that is identified as feminine. As in all learnings, the successful achievement of one task makes the accomplishment of the next related task easier. Failure in a task makes one unready for the next stage of development.

Modesty in regard to sex differences and sexual behavior, along with appropriate modesty in regard to elimination, are among the first major social learnings that the child will need as he leaves the exclusive family orientation and moves into a wider social world (17, p. 15; 17A, p. 12).

LEARNING TO RELATE ONESELF EMOTIONALLY
TO PARENTS, SIBLINGS, AND OTHER PEOPLE

Through the pleasure-pain, love-hate relationships, the infant starts to organize his feelings toward others. Through the anal and phallic periods, he learns to feel certain emotions toward people; he also learns how he *should* feel. The relationship between his actual feelings and the ones he is *supposed to have* serves as a major dynamic in character formation. The child has his basic lessons in expressing feelings or learning not to express them. He learns various ways of handling feelings that he may not express openly. Basic modes of emotional relationships toward various others are built during this period and will have an enduring effect upon his later life. This is a task that will be accomplished. The significant thing for future development is *how* it is accomplished (17, p. 16; 17A, p. 13).

FORMING SIMPLE CONCEPTS OF SOCIAL
AND PHYSICAL REALITY

Adults are likely to think of the world as there to be discovered by the infant and child. This is largely true; however, to some extent, the child creates his own perception of the world and checks it against evidences of the perception of others. He forms his own picture of the regularities and irregularities of the people and things around him. He uses the sequence of events to build a somewhat distorted picture of cause and effect, filling in with fantasy where reality does not suffice (17, p. 16; 17A, p. 13).

The child's view of reality is not taken in passively by isolated stimulation of the individual senses. It is built as part of an action-meaning system as the child interacts with the people and things in his environment. From the infant following a moving ring with his eyes to the five-year-old pushing and pulling a toy truck, it is the acting, doing, and manipulating functions that provide the test of reality.

In the social realm, concept formation about people—who they are and how they act—is not independent of the emotional relationships task. The child's concept of the social world is colored by his feelings about it. If, as some theorists contend, the child perceives *meanings* first, the first meanings are emotional; they refer to satisfaction and dissatisfaction of need (2). From this point of view, the child's first perceptions of mother are not of her as an independent person, but as comfort. Certain feelings of comfort and discomfort and mother mean the same thing. The child next differentiates the comfort from comforter, and mother attains a somewhat more independent existence. Yet, the initial feelings are instrumental in forming the concept and are never wholly separated from it. Similarly, as the child deals with other people and objects in his environment, it is first their emotional meaning, second their instrumental meaning, and only third their independent meaning that forms a concept structure of the world around him.

As language develops, the direct action in the immediate world can be expanded to indirect manipulation of words that refer to the world. As labels are applied and relationships are verbalized, the child can organize and stabilize his picture of the world more completely. By the time he goes to school, the child already has a fairly complete world view, on which he builds future learnings.

LEARNING TO DISTINGUISH RIGHT AND WRONG AND DEVELOPING A CONSCIENCE

All of the preceding tasks contribute to this one as the child, from his own feelings and the expression of people around him, forms value judgments about people, things, and events (17, p. 16; 17A, p. 13).

The verbalizing child will talk a great deal about "good" and "bad." He will label his own behavior and the behavior of other people and things. He builds a rather primitive system of values in which good and bad, right and wrong, are very important concepts. His overt behavior will not always be "good," but he is generally able to label "bad" behavior according to his own value system.

The discussion of superego development has indicated how some of the value material is repressed to the unconscious and forms an automatic governor of behavior. The conscience so developed protects the individual from having to make all decisions by a conscious reference to a value system. At the same time, it tends to be somewhat primitive and to retain the child's eye view of good and bad. The incorporated value systems of the parents, as the child sees them, will be somewhat distorted and may well conflict with later developments in his perception of reality. The child who responded to his mother's somewhat accusing question, "What are you doing?" with, "How can I do anything with you and God and Santa Claus all watching?" was being controlled by such a conscience.

The more conscious value system is more readily open to change and to differing interpretations of behavior. It is this phase of judgment about right and wrong that is available for elaboration as the child goes to school in the next stage of his development.

The end of the phallic period finds the troubled waters of personality development relatively calmed by resolution of conflict and repression. The basic personality is formed and the individual has the characteristics of id, ego, and superego in some kind of balance. He is freer now to turn his attention to the physical world and to social relationships beyond the family. With his energy less bound up in intrapersonal conflict, he can be more objective in his outlook. He is ready to explore other children, the wider community, the physical world, and his relations with other adults. Because of the relative psychic calm and the lack of crucial sexual events, the period from about six to the onset of adolescence is called the latent period. This does not mean that the child has lost interest in sex or that there are no emotional crises. It does mean that his energy is less bound up in intrapersonal conflict and can be used for other activities. It is a period for consolidation of the development that has taken place and for more objective appraisals (1, 8, 9, 10, 21). Paralleling this development, physical growth remains relatively constant until the preadolescent growth spurt. Growth in height

PSYCHOLOGICAL DEVELOPMENT: MIDDLE CHILDHOOD AND THE SCHOOL YEARS

11

and weight tend to be steady but proceed at a slower pace than in the first three or four years.

It is perhaps fortuitous but sound that in our culture this is the period when children venture into school. The latent period seems appropriate for the kind of function school can perform, perhaps better than the family. The child comes to school as a relatively complete individual personality. The school can provide for modifications, additions, and adaptations in that personality, but only in terms of its basic structure. The exception to this occurs in schools that are especially equipped to deal with malformed personalities and to provide appropriate therapy for rebuilding. Fundamental restructuring of personality is beyond the usual expectation for the typical American school.

ID EXPRESSION

The child's energy system expresses itself in play, physical activity, and social interaction. To the extent that it has been sublimated to curiosity and achievement orientation, it will be applied to intellectual activity and the accomplishment of school tasks. Building on these tendencies, the school provides channels to deepen and extend these socially approved modes of energy expenditure.

The child still needs time and opportunity to experiment with and to crystallize the modes of expression developed during the phallic period. The remnants of affection and hostility need release. In the early grades, the new adjustment to the mother and father prototype is tried out on teachers and modified in contact with peers (10, pp. 31-39). The initial relationship to kindergarten and first-grade teachers is more akin to love than to intellect. The typical kindergartner is emotionally responsive to going to school; however, many children who are still involved in the Oedipus conflict are terrified to leave home for fear of loss of a parent or of other terribly dangerous things that may happen.

EGO DEVELOPMENT

This is a rich period for the development of ego functions, especially in the areas of knowledge and intellectual activity. Even though he has been living for five or six years, the child is now, for the first time, free to devote his attention to the variegated world outside the family. He continues the process of distinguishing between fantasy and objective reality. He explores physical and social reality through his own direct experience, collects facts and information, and organizes these into some kind of order. He goes through a period of intensive interest in language in order to express his experiences, explore reality symbolically, and extend his experiences vicariously. He learns many skills to make his knowledge effective. As his picture of a complex objective world grows, he relates to it with a consequent differentiation of self and an increasingly definite self-concept (10, pp. 374-492).

A large part of this learning is social in that his wider contacts with others provide a laboratory for continuing motivation, for testing reality against others' concepts, and for getting a comparative picture of himself and his skills.

The structure and basic content of the superego have essentially been formed by the end of the phallic period. During latency, additional elaboration of concepts of right and wrong become attached to and woven into the moral fabric. The value system becomes increasingly sophisticated as more subtle distinctions and comparisons with reality are made. Some of this material is on a conscious level and is properly classed as ego function. Yet, much of it is rooted in the basic commands and prohibitions of the superego; it is less rational than ego material. We might suggest that the ego helps to *rationalize* the controls of the superego as behavior is tested against reality.

Conventionally, the American school adds to and strengthens the acculturated superego with its lessons on fair play, good sportsmanship, patriotism, thrift, and other applications of value concepts. The child who comes to school with a well-formed conventional superego is prepared to accept the teachings of the school and to elaborate his development with a minimum of conflict. On the other hand, the child who has incorporated parental values at variance with the school culture may find it impossible to accept and learn from the school. This may result in rebellion or extreme anxiety on the part of the child, to say nothing of the teacher's reaction. Where teachers and parents hold similar value positions and where these are consistent with those of the larger society, the course of superego development tends to run smoothly. Major variations lead to conflict that is both internal and manifested in external behavior (10, pp. 403-21).

112

DEVELOPMENTAL TASKS OF MIDDLE CHILDHOOD

Developmental tasks are never done. The tasks of infancy and early childhood give way to similar tasks in middle childhood (17, pp. 25-108). The ease or difficulty of these tasks is partly dependent upon how the earlier tasks were handled. The preceding description of the latent period provides a background for looking at how the child adapts himself to the new demands of society.

LEARNING PHYSICAL SKILLS NECESSARY FOR ORDINARY GAMES

Play is the major work of the young child (10, pp. 359-75). Through games, he develops his growing body and learns improved coordination of first large and then small muscle groups. He tries out rules and regulations governing social interaction. He elaborates concepts of fair play, competition, and cooperation. He tests himself out in play situations where success is important, but failure is not devastating. His play life contributes to his achievement of many of the developmental tasks of this period. Furthermore, in contemporary American culture, a continuing interest in sports and games is expected of adults and serves as an enrichment of adult life in an age of increasing leisure time. Central to all this is the rather complex learning of the physical skills necessary to engage in the ordinary games of childhood (17, p. 28; 17A, p. 15).

Typical American communities and the arrangement of living patterns for most children make this a relatively easy task. The relative regularity of physical growth sets the stage. Through school and after-school activities, the neighborhood play group, the provision of play space, and the availability of organized games, the child has the opportunity to move through a relatively well-graded curriculum of play. Typically, both self-interests and social pressures lead to normal accomplishment of the task.

However, there are individuals who are thwarted in this task and there are situations that limit its accomplishment. The child who goes through a lengthy illness or is otherwise kept out of action for a long period of time may miss critical learnings until it is too late to catch up. The child with a severe physical handicap may have to find and substitute another task, which keeps him out of the mainstream. Some parents and teachers restrict the child's play life unduly. Some communities or subgroups in communities may fail to provide the setting and stimulation for this task.

On the other hand, there are many situations where children's skills are exploited so that they are called on to perform and win before they have had a chance to learn and perfect the skill. Adult pressures, by demanding a degree of skill that children do not have, may interfere with the development of a normal level of skill. Some groups of children are so highly organized that only those who have the skills participate, and there is little opportunity for others to learn. To the extent that such situations interfere with all children achieving this task, they are psychologically harmful.

BUILDING WHOLESOME ATTITUDES TOWARD ONESELF
AS A GROWING ORGANISM

This task includes developing good health habits and positive attitudes toward health and the physical body. It also includes enjoyment of bodily activity and acceptance of the physical aspects of living (17, p. 29; 17A, p. 16).

On the individual level, the child must accept both his likeness with others and his own uniqueness. It is sometimes difficult for him to see himself as growing and changing. The child of six will become a very different physical organism at ten. Yet, his body image must be incorporated in his self-concept at both ages. Acceptance of the growing and changing self is not easy. The healthy child develops the concept, "I'm this big today, last year I was little, next year I'll be bigger."

Modern social arrangements probably make aspects of this task difficult. Children tend to be organized in homogeneous age groups. They typically have little intimate contact with younger and older children. A society of seven-year-olds has little opportunity for constant reference to what it was like to be younger and what it will be like to be older. Perhaps the large farm family and the one-room school of a previous generation provided a better setting for accomplishment of this task.

LEARNING TO GET ALONG WITH AGE MATES

The very arrangements that make the preceding task difficult facilitate this one. In both school and play group, children assemble with others of a similar developmental level. They have the opportunity to develop and try out social skills in a peer group in which no one is seriously disadvantaged. The standards of behavior are increasingly those demanded by the peer group, and the approval of age mates frequently carries more weight than the disapproval of parents and teachers (10, pp. 354-58; 17, p. 30; 17A, p. 17).

Much of the socialization function is taken over by the peer group as the child is inducted into the society of children by other children. This society seems to pass on from generation to generation a culture that adults have largely forgotten. If teachers taught nothing, but merely kept groups of children alive and undamaged, the child would still learn a great deal from his age-mate society.

Some of the games that children play and the verbalizations accompanying them in the form of chants and rhymes are not taught to them by adults. Nor do they invent them. There is a large repertory of games, superstitions, chants, schedules of activity, and convictions about the "right" way to do things that children learn from other children. Some of these are purely local, representing the traditions of an isolated time and place. Others have been transmitted in only slightly changed form from the distant past and from distant places. Children learn the right season for shooting marbles, for playing jacks. They jump rope and play "mumbly-peg" without instruction from adults. If we think back to our own childhood, we can recall some of the customs, activities, and folklore that were extant in our child society. Although adults sometimes do teach children games and activities from their own childhood and although toward the end of middle childhood the development of highly organized team sports is often increasingly controlled by adults, the society of age mates is in large part the controlling society, paralleling adult activities but separate from them. The child who adapts himself happily and successfully to the age-mate society is building strength for future tasks (25, 27, pp. 206-24).

LEARNING AN APPROPRIATE MASCULINE
OR FEMININE SOCIAL ROLE

This is a continuation of earlier tasks and is built upon the basic sex-role identification, which was made earlier. The distinctive feature for this period is that it is essentially concerned with the social role, rather than the emotional or sexual aspects of earlier and later periods. The task is carried out in association with age mates and in contact with adults (17, p. 32; 17A, p. 19).

Although there is intermingling of the sexes, there is a strong tendency for boys and girls to pull apart and associate with their own sex groups. This separation, especially in play groups, tends to be important about age eight or nine. These are the same age groups that form informal clubs and "secret societies," with rituals and passwords stressing their exclusive qualities. It is also the period when the child is likely to put great importance on having a "best friend" of the same sex (10, pp. 318-25, 354-58).

All of this activity has the effect of causing the child to adapt his behavior to that of others of the same sex, for the boy to learn to do the things that boys do and for the girl to accept approved feminine activities. The group of children can be quite insistent on appropriate behavior and quite intolerant of the boy or girl who does not conform.

At the same time, adults in the child's experience are serving as models of masculine and feminine behavior and are expanding the role concepts the child has established with his parents. They also give approval and disapproval to activities judged according to sex typing.

As the child becomes capable of profiting from vicarious experiences, books, movies, and television also provide models for correct behavior as a boy or a girl.

There is considerable concern expressed in some segments of our society that these various forces are tending toward a feminization of behavior. Typically, there are more female figures than male figures exerting direct influence on boys and girls. A great majority of teachers in elementary schools are women. Approved behavior in school tends to follow modes traditionally thought of as feminine.

There are corresponding changes in adult society. The modern image of marriage relationships has a less differentiated social sex role than that of previous generations. The concept of a cooperative partnership between husband and wife is increasingly accepted. The traditional masculine virtues of aggressiveness and dominance and the feminine virtue of submissiveness are less valued. Perhaps the goals of the task may be changing, but its nature remains the same.

ACHIEVING PERSONAL INDEPENDENCE FROM PARENTS AND OTHER ADULTS

The child must become an autonomous person, taking responsibility for his own behavior, planning his own activities, and making his own decisions. This autonomy is never complete independence; however, in our culture, it should imply increasing self-direction (17, p. 38; 17A, p. 25).

At the beginning of the latency period, the child may still see his parents as omniscient and almost omnipotent. He transfers some of this attitude to his teacher when he goes to school. "Teacher said" may be the ultimate proof of truth. Somewhere in the course of development he discovers that parents and teachers make mistakes, that there are things they do not know. He may also discover that there are things he knows better than a particular adult. There comes a shift from the authority of others in knowledge to the authority of his own experience (10, pp. 326-53).

This is true in other areas of living. Increasingly, the child helps to plan and make decisions. He moves farther from adults into his own world. If this independence is built successfully, there will be less need for rebellion in adolescence when this task assumes additional qualities.

DEVELOPING FUNDAMENTAL SKILLS IN READING, WRITING, AND CALCULATING

This is the task modern society has largely turned over to the school. Although the school makes its contributions to the other tasks, its role is central in this one. American society is a highly verbal society. Getting around in the modern world requires a minimum ability to read street signs and follow simple directions. Writing is required for simple communication and the recording of ideas. The manipulation of number skills is necessary for minimum economic welfare. Higher levels of participation in modern life require corresponding increases in these skills. For most people who attend school, the basic skills required for getting along in everyday life are mastered by the end of the elementary-school period. In actuality, the skill level acquired by the average third-grader is adequate for the everyday needs of adult life. Much higher levels are usually attained (17, p. 33; 17A, p. 20).

Reading, writing, and calculating are not isolated processes. The child starts to learn to read when he learns the process of labelling things and first begins to derive meaning from hearing others talk and begins to talk himself. He is becoming ready for reading as he builds a background of experience to which labels can be applied. Only arbitrarily can we pick a particular point in the process before or after which we can say that Johnny can't or can read. It would be more accurate to describe the level of the reading process he has attained. The most advanced readers can still improve certain of their reading skills.

Children come to school with different levels of readiness for reading instructions. This readiness is a complex matter involving physical development, emotional maturity, breadth of experience, attitudes toward learning, and language development. The same is true for writing and for working with numbers. The way the school helps the child master this task through the years of middle childhood will have profound influences upon all other tasks of the same and later periods (10, pp. 374-402).

DEVELOPING CONCEPTS NECESSARY FOR EVERYDAY LIVING

This is a school-related task, but it is also a continuation of the earlier task of forming concepts. The child comes to school with a large number of concepts already formed. By the end of the elementary-school period, these will be expanded enormously and refined extensively. In early childhood, concepts were built from direct experience and were embedded in their emotional context. In middle childhood, a more objective elaboration occurs and thinking activity becomes less dependent on immediate direct experience. The child also becomes increasingly able to deal with higher levels of abstraction. Intellectual curiosity develops in its own right and the child wants to find out what things are, how they work, what causes what, how things fit together. For most children, this interest is focussed more on the impersonal aspects of the world than on human relationships. Human relationships are given and are experienced directly. The other aspects of the world are investigated and thought about. The child seems to be seeking an orderliness and predictability in the world about him, and much of his curiosity is used to that end (17, p. 34; 17A, p. 21).

It may be useful to think of concepts as having three dimensions defined by three questions—what?, how?, why? In general, the *what* is derived first from personal direct observation and experience. Additional content is built by extending language referring to the direct experience and applying it by analogy to the nonpresent experience. Thus, the concept behind the label "high mountain" may be built directly for the child who lives in sight of Pikes Peak. For the child who has never been anywhere except the plains of Iowa, the concept will have to be built synthetically out of a variety of other experiences. The *how* questions go beyond direct experience and require the mental manipulation of concrete facts. The child is likely to go through a period of collecting, classifying, categorizing, and making lists of things in order to establish relationships and see how things go together. He must eventually go beyond the surface appearance of things and postulate events he can not observe in order to answer the *how* questions. The *why* questions demand an even higher level of abstraction, as the child seeks reasons that are more general explanations of the world around him.

Investigations of the properties of things, of the processes working in the world, and of the explanations behind phenomena take a great deal of the time and energy of the school-age child. By the end of childhood, the learner has a serviceable store of concepts, which enable him to get along in a relatively predictable world and to communicate with others on a basis of relatively common concepts (17, pp. 77-91).

DEVELOPING ATTITUDES TOWARD SOCIAL GROUPS AND INSTITUTIONS

As the child develops and refines concepts, he builds value judgments and emotional response qualities related to them. The web of prejudices, belief systems, response tendencies, and feelings toward school, church, government, other countries, "American ideals," religion, minority groups, and a great variety of other institutions, ideas, and peoples are well developed by the time the child leaves the elementary school. These can be changed later, but are highly resistant to changes other than strengthening or specific application (17, p. 40; 17A, p. 27).

Attitudes are developed in several ways. Identification and imitation have been described in the character-building process of early childhood. The same kind of process, without as deep an emotional involvement, continues in middle childhood as the child adopts the perceived feelings of significant adults, teacher and others, and of significant peers in the child society. As before, the rejection of the attitudes of disliked persons is part of the process. The figures for identification need not be real or living persons. Much attitude formation comes through identification with fictional and historical figures presented by stories, books, television, films, and other mass media.

Where the significant figures in a child's environment present a consistent set of attitudes with a minimum of conflicts, the child's attitude will be an easily formed reflection of this situation. Where there are serious inconsistencies or conflicts in and among significant persons, the task will be more difficult and its outcome less predictable.

Attitudes are also built through extreme emotional experiences, in which the emotional arousal attaches itself to an event or class of events and is generalized to a large number of events perceived as similar. Unexpected attitudes are sometimes developed through such reactions to critical events.

A third way of viewing attitude formation includes both of the others, but sees attitudes built out of the gradual accumulation of feelings, pleasant and unpleasant, which accompany a category of experience. Thus, the particular nature and quality of an individual's patriotism, for example, is a resultant of many experiences associated with geographical, historical, national, and social concepts. The attitudes thus formed will provide the bias which permits future learning and action.

It is obvious that the school, the home, the play group, and individual relationships and events all contribute to the attitudes toward social groups and institutions with which the individual leaves the childhood period.

DEVELOPING CONSCIENCE, MORALITY,
AND A SCALE OF VALUES

It has been emphasized that the conscience developed in early childhood tends to be primitive. It blindly categorizes good and bad or right and wrong. Part of the task of middle childhood is to make this conscience more subtle and to make its application to behavior more sophisticated. The child of ten is more judicious in his condemnation or approval of the behavior of himself and others than is the child of six. As the child moves into the wider world and away from the family, as he builds concepts about the wider world, as he becomes aware of the varied behavior of people, he must build wider referents for the judgment of good and bad. The application of such judgments provides additional content for the conscience (10, pp. 422-51; 17, p. 36; 17A, p. 23).

At the same time, more conscious and rational judgment about the consequences of behavior are compared with the commands and prohibitions of conscience. In our society, it is desirable for the authoritarian morality of conscience to be modified in the direction of a morality of assent and cooperation. As the child apprehends rules and regulations in games, peer relationships, family, and classroom, he is enabled to move toward such a morality. The perception of rules seems to follow a course that demonstrates this movement. At first, the child behaves as though the game rules are absolute, invariable, and given. Later he experiments with making up rules for new games. Eventually, he sees that rules are conventions, agreed upon to form the boundaries of any given game, which can be changed through proper procedures. This same process is applied, to some degree, in the more complex activities of life; and the child increasingly governs his behavior by a conscious morality.

The third phase of this task, developing a scale of values, will be far from complete by the end of childhood. The individual will still be struggling with this task well into adulthood; however, it is well begun in the elementary-school years. As decisions about behavior and values are made, a rough scale of the comparative importance of various areas develops. A hierarchy of values is applied and tested in further decisions.

SUBCULTURAL AND INDIVIDUAL DIFFERENCES IN THE DEVELOPMENTAL TASKS

The description of developmental tasks for a child looking toward adulthood in Russia or South Africa would obviously have features quite different from the preceding descriptions. Similar areas would undoubtedly be considered, but goals and details of the process would be altered. The very nature of the developmental-task concept assumes a particular society. The description here given assumes the pressures of American middle-class society in mid-twentieth century. There are many individual interpretations of that society, and there are many subcultures in American society. The demands and expectations placed on children vary. There are shifting variations in the values of social classes, religious groups, and regional identifications. One result of combining the dominant value system with these differences is the value placed on change, flexibility, and adaptability. In a more monolithic society, the tasks would be more definite and more rigid. In our society, they are more subject to change.

Consequently, the developmental tasks in our culture are perhaps best thought of as wide roadways, rather than as straight and narrow paths. There is considerable room for deviation without interrupting the journey, yet there is pressure to move along the road. The destination cannot even be perceived, except in very general terms. Progress can be estimated only by checking certain milestones along the way.

To continue the metaphor, the road is narrower in earlier stages, and becomes increasingly wide as development proceeds. In other words, the tasks of infancy are more definite, more easily defined, and more susceptible to evaluation. In adulthood, there are more alternatives, more possible variations, and more acceptable specific differences in the accomplishment of broad developmental tasks. The next stage of growth gives evidence of this.

The tides of physical and psychological development shift at about the age of twelve. The latent period opens into a new genital orientation, and the characteristics of physical development accelerate toward maturity. Adolescence is technically defined as the period between puberty and maturity. This definition is not as simple as it appears, because the two defining terms are from different realms of discourse. Puberty is a biological term indicating sexual readiness to beget or bear offspring. It indicates a physiological change in the body such that, for the first time, the male is capable of impregnating and the female of being impregnated. Maturity is a much more complex term connoting, in this context, readiness for adult life in all its emotional, social, economic, and legal aspects.

In common usage, which will be followed here, adolescence commonly includes part of a prepubertal period, starting with the body changes that herald the onset of puberty. This period is referred to as the pubescent period. The term "adolescence" in the following discussion is not precisely defined, but includes the period slightly prior to puberty to a variable time signalling adulthood.

It is possible to conceive of a society in which maturity might follow so closely upon puberty

PSYCHOLOGICAL DEVELOPMENT: ADOLESCENCE AND THE GENITAL PERIOD

12

that adolescence would be a very brief period (approximately two years), during which physical maturation would take place.

In our society, the demands for maturity are such that adolescence is typically extended well beyond the point that physical development alone would indicate. At both the beginning and end of adolescence, social expectations are more compelling than physiological change itself. Socially, adolescence begins as the end of childhood, with demands for different kinds of behavior. It ends when the person takes his place in the society of adults, a time that will vary from individual to individual. The tension between biological development and social pressures is again the significant psychological factor.

PHYSICAL DEVELOPMENT

Prior to puberty, there is a change in glandular functions, which affects the growth of the body. The rate of growth in height, for most individuals, starts to increase before puberty is achieved, reaches its peak at puberty, and then declines till its cessation some four or five years later. For some individuals, slight increments in height are continued for several more years. Hence, the individual enters adolescence with a rapidly changing body as judged by the most obvious measure, change in size.

There are fundamental differences in the two sexes in the growth curves of this period. The average girl, with wide individual differences, reaches the peak velocity and starts the decline in rate between twelve and thirteen. The average boy, with equally wide individual differences, is approximately two years behind the girl. The boy, at his peak, is typically gaining more than the girl at hers. For the only time in their lives, typical boys are smaller than typical girls of the same age between ten and a half and thirteen years. In the year of greatest growth, the average girl gains about an inch and a half in height, the boy approximately two inches. The average, of course, implies wide individual differences. On the average, adult males will be about 10 per cent taller and heavier than adult females (15, pp. 417-21).

The reproductive organs, internal and external, undergo their greatest growth and change at this time. From the earliest growth period, the body tissues comprising the reproductive organs grow relatively slowly, reaching less than 20 per cent of their adult volume by the age of four or five years. They grow no more until about the age of twelve when, under the influence of the differential effects of hormonal changes, they achieve adult proportions by almost straight-line growth of reproductive tissue over the next eight years.

At about the age of twelve (younger for girls, older for boys), there is greater internal growth disparity in the physical organism than at any other time before or after this period. The nonreproductive glandular tissues of the lymphoid type, though small in proportion to the rest of the body mass, are almost twice as large as they will be at maturity. They will actually decrease in amount by the age of twenty. Brain and head tissues have achieved approximately their full size, and are out of adult proportion only because the rest of the body has not yet caught up. The general body type follows the general curve as described for height; at about the age of twelve, it is at a relatively low point, starting a period of rapid increase. The reproductive tissues are just ready to begin their rapid change. Between twelve and twenty, a very differently proportioned body will develop (15, pp. 417-32).

The growth of reproductive tissue signals the physiological sexual maturity that starts the menstrual cycle in females and prepares the sperm and genital organs of the male for their part in reproduction. These changes are equally definite in both sexes, but are far more dramatic in the case of the girl. Changes directly related to these events are referred to as *primary-sex* characteristics. Accompanying changes in appearance, which further differentiate males and females (such as facial hair), are referred to as *secondary-sex* characteristics. These changes appear to be hereditary (in both the species and individual sense) in the sequence in which the changes occur; however, they are modifiable in terms of long-range environmental influence in regard to the rate and timing of their occurrence. Thus, there is evidence that starvation retards sexual developments and causes the body to wait longer for physiological changes. There is also some evidence that puberty is occurring slightly earlier in the United States in recent generations as compared to earlier ones. It is possible that our higher standards of nourishment and increasing physical growth rate are related to this.

It may be interesting to note the sequence and general time of appearance of both primary- and secondary-sex characteristics, throughout adolescence. Because the girl's development is both more dramatic and earlier, this is described first. The ages given are averages, with some indication of the observed range of expected differences. There are rare cases where these ranges are widely extended, as in such pathological situations as precocious puberty in boys as young as age four or five or in the recorded case of a girl of five giving birth to a child by Caesarian section. These rare cases are apparently so pathological that healthy development is not possible. The ranges given here are well within the bounds of potential satisfactory adjustment.

At about the age of eleven (as early as eight for some girls, as late as thirteen for others), the breast starts to enlarge and develop. This is usually the first sign of sexual development. This growth process is completed in about two and a half years. At about the same time, but usually following the beginning of breast growth, pubic hair develops and reaches its mature state at about fourteen (eleven for early maturers, seventeen for late maturers). The rapid increase in height starts at the same time, reaches its peak at about twelve, and levels off before fourteen. The peak may come as early as ten or as late as fourteen and a half. These changes are climaxed by the menarche, the first menstrual period, at about thirteen and a half (ranging from ten to sixteen and a half). The girl is usually still infertile for a year or eighteen months after menarche, so that conception can take place at about eleven plus at the earliest and not earlier than eighteen for some.

The sequence of events for the boy is similar, though typically starting later and developing more slowly. Nor are the changes as visible until the latter part of the pubertal cycle, when the secondary-sex characteristics give phenotypical evidence of manhood. At about twelve (ten for early maturers, thirteen and a half for late) the testes and scrotum begin accelerated growth reaching maximum development four years later. At the same time, pubic hair begins to lengthen, coarsen, and develop more pigmentation. This process is relatively slow, continuing past the conclusion of the more definitive changes. The beginnings of rapid increase in height and the growth of the penis start at the same time, age thirteen on the average. The height spurt starts as early as ten and a half for some and as late as sixteen for others. The corresponding ranges for penis growth are eleven and fourteen and a half, with the completion of adult size and development of the penis occurring about four years after its initiation (15, pp. 430-32).

Though starting later than the girl, the boy's increase in height is greater and continues longer, reaching its peak at an average of fourteen years and tapering off more slowly. The growth of the larynx and consequent deepening of the voice follows the pattern of penis growth. Facial hair develops slowly, starting with the hair at the corners of the upper lip, and becoming a full beard (according to individual genetic constitution) only by the end of the pubertal cycle.

It should be noted that the sequence of events is consistent, that the early maturer tends to enter each event of the sequence sooner and complete it sooner than the average. The late maturer may not only enter the cycle later, but may take slightly longer to complete it. Hence, some individuals may have completed the full sequence of physically mature development before others of the same chronological age show any evidence of beginning the process of change toward maturity (15, pp. 417-32).

To put this in statistical terms, perhaps 1 per cent of boys and 20 per cent of girls will be in the pubertal cycle at age eleven and a half. By thirteen and a half, 5 per cent of boys and 50 per cent of girls can be considered physically mature. At this time, 60 per cent of boys and 15 per cent of girls have not yet entered the pubertal cycle. By seventeen and a half, approximately 90 per cent of boys and 100 per cent of girls can be classed as physically mature.

This description has emphasized time and events in the sequence of change. It should be realized, however, that the process is continuous, gradual, and extended over a considerable period of time. For most young people, the subjective experiencing of change is attenuated. With the exception of menarche in the girl, there is no single event that can suddenly be perceived as marking the achievement of puberty or maturity. The landmarks of growth can usually be seen only retrospectively. The individual is usually not aware of many of the changes or of the magnitude of change. Although the change is dramatic if it is viewed as a discontinuous before and after picture at ten and eighteen, it is not necessarily sudden or traumatic, except as culture or the emotional climate make it so.

Psychosexual development enters a new phase at the beginning of adolescence. The quiescence of emotionally laden sex concerns during latency must give way to a valueing of genital sexual activity. By the end of adolescence, the individual must have come to terms with adult expressions of sexuality.

Some of the necessity for a new adjustment comes from the biological changes described above. The internal body changes and concomitant maturing of the sexual organs give new strength and potential to impulse life. The biological possibility of true sexual fulfillment psychologically affects the individual's emotional reservoir and manifests itself in greater overt emotional responsiveness. The labile nature of the changes produces varying emotional responsiveness.

At the same time, in our culture, the social pressures and expectations of others change. New demands are put upon the individual, necessitating rather major adjustments. The childish adjustment established at the beginning of latency is no longer satisfactory, and a reorganization of the self must take place. The sublimations of libido that were constructive for childhood outgrow their usefulness, and some of the repressed material that made them possible can no longer be held down. There must be a rearousal of some aspects of the Oedipus complex if the transition to mature love relationships is to be established. A rearousal of phallic interests is necessary in order to transform sexuality into a true genital form with acceptable love objects as its aim. The degree of difficulty in making this transition will depend upon the nature of the earler adjustment, present demands of the life situation, and the clarity of future goals. Some adolescents make the transition very smoothly with none of the "storm and stress" that western tradition has seen in adolescence. For others, it is a stormy period or an anxiety-ridden process with many violent shifts involved in readjustment (1, 8, 9, 13).

The eight-year-old who says, "I hate girls, and I'm never going to get married" is behaving quite acceptably. By eighteen, his attitude should change considerably! There must be changes in id, ego, and superego and in their interaction to bring about this transformation.

ID EXPRESSION

During latency, the id has functioned in the service of the ego and its work of dealing with objective reality. In adolescence, its impulses turn toward the pleasures of genital expression. The sexual organs are, in a sense, rediscovered, and their pleasure-giving propensities re-explored. With physical maturation, these pleasure-giving qualities are enhanced.

There is considerable evidence that masturbation increases in early adolescence, more extensively among boys than among girls (13, pp. 287-91). The genital outlet of temporary homosexual relationships is relatively common. The drive for sexual activity most appropriately seeks a heterosexual object; however, in a society that officially disapproves of premarital sexual relationships, this aim is frequently thwarted.

Partly as a result of this thwarting, and for other reasons, much of the libidinal energy is channeled into cross-sex-social relationships, rather than achieving direct expression. In contemporary American society, the games of childhood are extended into a more libidinous social game known as "dating." The id also expends its energy in partial sublimations, such as in the activities and group competitions of adolescent society known as high school or college life (3).

There may also be a change in emotional responsiveness related to the increased id activity. Some adolescents display intense emotional reactions to everyday situations. Others seem to lose normal emotional response and to handle situations with a quality of emotional flatness. In still others, there may be an alternation of these extremes. Seldom does the adolescent continue to display the same emotional response quality that was characteristic of his childhood (13, pp. 329-54).

By the end of adolescence, the healthy individual will have moved from the relative sexual repression of latency, through the stage of primary-genital gratification, to the capability of receiving gratification with a member of the opposite sex in a mutual relationship that is gratifying to both partners. Anything less than this is not a satisfactory resolution of the adolescent stage in our culture. Thus, the overt homosexual or the "sexual athlete," though obtaining libidinal gratification, remains to some extent an adolescent and does not progress fully to maturity.

In the process of releasing the energy of the id for direct sexual expression, the earlier solution of the Oedipus conflict is no longer satisfactory. Emotional relationships with parents undergo some changes, which may express themselves in various ways. The love-hate dyad, which has been partially submerged, is now reasserted. To a large extent, the emotional relationship between parents and the younger adolescent is more a function of the nature of the earlier relationship among them than it is a question of current activities. The overt behavior of the adolescent toward his parents is a resultant of many complex factors of which this new emotional relationship is one.

125

SUPEREGO FUNCTIONS AND DEVELOPMENT

As the newly maturing sexual responses become possible, their actual forms of expression are partly governed by the strength and nature of the superego. If strong specific prohibitions about sexual feelings and sexual activities have been built in, the new adjustment will be difficult. If the prohibitions have been more general, they may be reinterpreted more easily. If the Oedipus situation has been solved through an acceptance of potential sexual activity with a non-parent-opposite-sex person, there may be little prohibition and few guilt feelings about sexual experimentation.

In other areas of living, such as engaging in adolescent social activities, preparing for vocational competition, or separating from parents, other commands and prohibitions of superego will affect adolescent behavior. When an adolescent rebels violently against his parents, he may be expressing a resentment of his own superego controls. If so, he will feel even more guilty than the situation requires after the outburst.

On the other hand, the individual with minimal superego controls may have little protection against his own impulses, whose free expression is prohibited by our society. An extremely delicate balance between the forces described as id and those described as superego is necessary for healthy passage through adolescence.

During adolescence, the id and the ego are expanding. The individual's task in relation to the superego is to reduce it, at least in its unconscious aspects. The mature individual exerts a higher proportion of rational control of his behavior and is less subject to the blind control of a childish value system. This task will be defined further in the discussion of developmental tasks in adolescence.

EGO DEVELOPMENT

As the mediating function between reality and the total organism, the ego goes through a tremendous expansion during adolescence. The impulsive demands of the id must be dealt with in the context of superego commands. The world continues to expand as it did in childhood, but now the individual's relationship to the expanding world is different. By the end of adolescence, the individual is expected to be an independent contributing unit in that world. It is no longer enough to discover the world; it must be acted upon.

In the intellectual realm, the individual is more capable of dealing with abstract ideas; many adolescents seem to take pleasure in the process of reasoning. A growing sensitivity to the feelings and rights of others impels more interest in social and psychological matters on an intellectual level. The concern about things and their relationship, which was characteristic of latency, gives way to concerns about the "why" of human behavior and interpersonal relationships. The theory behind things may become more important than the thing itself.

Part of this intellectual activity seems to be in the service of a more definite and differentiated self-concept. Associations among teenagers are used both as comparisons on which to model behavior and as support for the behavior and the picture of self it projects. Frequently, the self-concept formed in adolescence, realistic or unrealistic, is carried over into early adulthood and governs basic adjustment.

Finally, the ego has the difficult task of finding socially acceptable ways of permitting id gratifications and of incorporating these into its total action system in ways that fit the demands of a complex, real world.

DEVELOPMENTAL TASKS OF ADOLESCENCE

As the individual moves toward adulthood, the demands of society attain greater priority over the internal needs of the person. The developmental tasks of adolescence, therefore, help prepare the individual for adult life to a greater extent than did those of childhood. As always, success in the tasks implies the use of the nature and needs of the individual in furthering the accomplishment of societal demands. The tasks are arranged here in a rough order from the more personal to the more societal.

Physical beauty and a healthy physique are highly valued in our culture, along with a concept of the possibility of self-improvement in physical attractiveness. The adolescent's estimate of his future status, as well as of his present condition, is important in building a self-concept and setting goals for the future (17, p. 120; 17A, p. 39).

Athletic activities are highly valued in the adolescent subculture (3). Success or failure in these are partly dependent on the physical body itself, and they have great influence on the individual's picture of himself. We have a tradition of adolescence as the "awkward age." Yet, all tests of actual physical skill show a steady development. If anything, there tends to be an increase in athletic abilities reaching its peak shortly after the peak of the growth spurt. The alleged awkwardness is more a social phenomenon, related to the wider social activities of adolescence that place the individual in many new situations, which he has not yet learned to handle with his changing body. He is still learning to use his body effectively.

The demands of adults and acceptance by the group operate differently with different impact on the early and late maturer. Both are out of phase with the average of the age group, but the acceptance of the particular physique is quite a different task for each of them.

A number of observations and studies indicate that the early maturing boy (during early adolescence) is, of course, taller, heavier, and physically more able than his contemporaries. Personally and socially, he also tends to be superior, in the sense that his behavior is more like that of an older person. He tends to be more popular, exerts more leadership, and is more self-contained and confident. In other words, personality characteristics tend to follow physical growth more than they do age trends. The late maturing boy, at the same period of time, tends to be more childish in his behavior patterns, slower to adopt the social interests of his age group, and indicates some sense of inferiority. There is some evidence that these personality differences persist into adulthood (23, pp. 32-45).

The adjustment of early and late maturing girls in an age-grouped society is somewhat different. Because pubescence normally sets in earlier for girls than for boys, the early maturing girl will be comparatively far ahead of her age mates. She may be completely mature physically for five or six years before the last maturing boy of the same age catches up. Her psychological growth can seldom match her physical growth, and she has difficulty with the intellectual and behavioral expectations that may be put upon her. The late maturing girl may have greater advantages in a culture that lengthens adolescence as ours does. She better fits the cultural demands. Yet, she may be so far behind her age group that social adjustment is difficult. The evidence is not clear on the relative adult adjustment of these two extremes (23, pp. 45-52).

The extremes of early and late maturing dramatize this developmental task. The example of the early maturing boy illustrates the probability of a fairly easy acceptance of his physique and the use of that acceptance in positive personality development. It is difficult for the late maturer to perceive and really believe that he will "catch up," that he will be "normal." Because time of maturing is related to body type, the late maturer will probably be in better condition in middle age, tending less to fat and maintaining a more youthful appearance.

Parents and teachers might help with this task by helping to project growth curves, thereby helping with more realistic predictions of future status.

ACHIEVING NEW AND MORE MATURE RELATIONS WITH AGE MATES OF BOTH SEXES

From same sex "secret" clubs of ten-year-olds, through mixed sex crowd and dating behavior, to adult social relationships and engagement or marriage is a long transition and requires many transformations. Friendships become both more varied and of longer duration. Where the child tended to form friendships on the basis of propinquity, the adolescent is more likely to seek friends with common interests (17, p. 111; 17A, p. 33).

Each generation of adolescents seems to form its own society with its own mores and customs, including distinctive language patterns. Such societies tend to be rather rigid in their standards of approved and acceptable behavior. Increasingly, this society is separated from the adult society and is the arbiter of values and behavior for its members (3).

The development of such a society is frequently viewed with alarm by adults. Yet, it serves as a mechanism whereby the age-mate relationship is structured and serves as the base for several other developmental tasks. In an industrial society characterized by change, direct transmission of unchanged parental values is not functional. The adolescent society serves as an intermediary for the changes that will be required of the young adult. Successful adaptation to adolescent society serves as a prototype for later adjustments to changing adult society.

ACHIEVING A MASCULINE OR FEMININE SOCIAL ROLE

The adolescent society also sets the tone for dating behavior and forms the codes of relationships between the sexes. The social role of one sex in relation to the other expands enormously as compared to the relationships of childhood. In this area, there is much new learning (17, p. 115; 17A, p. 37).

In relationship to adults and in everyday activities and interests, the sex-typed social role has been rather well learned during childhood. The adolescent task is to achieve this role in expanded social relations. The teenager must try his interpretation of the role on a more nearly adult level. There is likely to be a great deal of evaluation of self and others, with perhaps excessive embarrassment about temporary failures.

ACHIEVING EMOTIONAL INDEPENDENCE OF PARENTS AND OTHER ADULTS

This is one of the central tasks of adolescents. In our society (unlike some others), the young adult separates from his parents and starts an independent family of his own. To be ready to achieve this, he must become emotionally independent during adolescence. As a young adult, he is expected to "stand on his own two feet." It is not as customary in our society as in some to continue to depend on the family of origin (17, p. 123; 17A, p. 42).

A healthy achievement in this task requires some subtle readjustments of values and feelings. Ideally, the outcome should be a feeling of affection and respect for parents without emotional dependence on them. As an adult among adults, the individual should be able to respect others and be deserving of their respect. Yet, we anticipate that this will be a mutual rather than a dependent relationship.

Achieving emotional independence is complicated by many factors. First, economic dependence is likely to continue past the time when emotional dependence is appropriate. Second, the adolescent is likely to feel some guilt or anxiety on severing the emotional ties that have sustained him. Third, the middle-aged parents are facing some developmental tasks of their own, which may make it difficult for them to relinquish the satisfactions received from their children's emotional ties. Fourth, emotional independence depends to some extent on shifting the emotional relationship to other appropriate persons, where it can be more mutual and less dependent.

Little wonder then, that the relationship between parents and teenagers is frequently stormy and fraught with mutual misunderstandings. Many arguments may take place, for example, about the use of the family car, which are not about the car at all. The car may well be a symbol of independence and quite unimportant in itself. Sometimes the most submissive teenager may be furious inside at his dependence and desire to break away. Earlier conflicts that have not truly been resolved may be reinstituted in the struggle over this task (9, pp. 270-85; 13, pp. 383-420).

When both parents and adolescent have accomplished their other developmental tasks well up to this point, the granting of independence and the achieving of it may go smoothly. However, more usually, there is some conflict.

The existence of adolescent society provides a number of devices that help in this task. By identifying with the group and its values, the adolescent finds a temporary substitute between parental dependence and dependence on self. The standards and loyalties provided by others give the adolescent support in giving up his dependence on adults before he is ready for independence. The emotional relationship with the opposite sex is given form and substance under the sanction and surveillance of the teenage subculture.

PREPARING FOR MARRIAGE AND FAMILY LIFE

In a sense, all the developmental tasks contribute to this one. Attitudes toward self and others, appropriate emotional responses, differentiated social roles, and tasks related to vocational life are all necessary components to the successful achievement of this task. Its achievement is complicated by the implication that we must prepare for marriage and family life, but we must delay it for some time after we are prepared. The increasing frequency of teenage marriages may require a reanalysis of this task (17, p. 133; 17A, p. 52).

The expectation in this area is basically the development of a positive attitude toward marriage and the raising of a family. These attitudes result in realistic anticipation of marriage in the future. Along with these attitudes goes the orientation of many activities toward becoming ready for marriage.

Starting before adolescence, typical attitudes toward marriage are reported by boys and girls (13, pp. 375-82). At ten, a majority of girls and fewer boys expect to marry someday. This is generalized, and commonly no specific person is considered as a mate. The emphasis, especially for girls, is on the number of children desired rather than on marriage as such.

By twelve, there is little change except that more boys definitely say they will remain bachelors. At thirteen, very few plan to remain bachelors; however, there is still little concern about a particular spouse. The number of children desired typically has increased. Fourteen-year-olds seem less decisive about marriage, though most girls still expect to get married. By fifteen, there appears to be more interest in the characteristics of a particular spouse.

At least one interview study indicates that boys of sixteen are more undecided about marriage; they show less spontaneous acceptance of the conventional agreement that "of course one marries" (13, p. 382). This may indicate that the question of marriage starts to become more individual, intimate, and realistic at about this time.

By eighteen or twenty, attitudes toward marrying are fairly well set. It appears that after this time, basic changes in this attitude are difficult.

ACHIEVING ASSURANCE OF ECONOMIC INDEPENDENCE

Like the preceding task, this one is preparatory rather than completed. It implies understanding oneself and one's potentialities well enough to relate them to the world of work and to feel realistically confident of one's chances of making a living in the world (17, p. 127; 17A, p. 45).

In our culture, a high priorty is given to the value of productive work and economic independence. Yet, we do a poor job of providing ways for adolescents to meet this task. More institutional arrangements exist to keep the adolescent from working and earning money than exist to help him. The adolescent is kept economically dependent on his family long after he could be ready to earn at least some money. Unlike the farmhome of the last century, today's homes typically provide little useful work whereby the adolescent can contribute constructively. It may be that increasing family prosperity further restricts opportunities to do truly useful work and develop positive attitudes toward economic independence.

Paralleling these blocks toward independence is a continued increase in the material standard of living and the young person's expectations; for example, he expects his first home in his anticipated married life to have all the conveniences.

Although our institutions are not geared to the easy accomplishment of this task during adolescence, there are jobs an adolescent can do to feel useful and to assess his economic potential. A good example is the development of the practice of "baby-sitting," which scarcely existed two generations ago. Contemporary adolescents have built this into a major service and a major source of income, which contributes a great deal to achievement of this task.

Along with achieving assurance of economic independence, the adolescent must clarify vocational goals and start moving toward them (17, p. 128; 17A, p. 47).

Before ten, talk of careers is likely to be unrealistic, extrapolated from childish interests, and tending to follow glamorous images. By ten, a little more realism appears; by eleven, many will have a single definite career choice. By twelve, the trend toward realism continues with fairly definite career choices, but also with the verbalized recognition that "I may change my mind." More definite is the listing of the things the twelve-year-old does *not* want to do. The typical thirteen-year-old is likely to make a single definite choice of future occupation and to be somewhat firm about it.

This definiteness breaks down by fourteen. Career choice is expanding and occupations not previously mentioned are considered for future vocations. This indefiniteness continues in fifteen-year-olds, with an expansion of ideas into a field of work rather than a definite job. By sixteen, the general area of future work is likely to be fairly well decided. In a majority of cases, this choice is fairly realistic and sufficiently firm to provide a start toward the world of work (13, pp. 375-82).

The majority of choices are somewhat conventional. The adolescent does not have the experience with the expanding field of vocations or the assurance of his own abilities to foresee the variety of possibilities. In a society in which occupational possibilities are changing and expanding, adequate accomplishment of this task is extremely difficult. Our society demands a delicate balance of preparing for a definite occupation and becoming flexible enough to accept and adjust to vocational mobility. In his life span, the adolescent in school today will see thousands of jobs created that never existed before. He will also see many current vocational opportunities vanish under automation and industrial change.

There are three areas of learning involved in this task: first, an assessment of interest in types of occupations and specific occupations; second, an orientation to and an understanding of the world of work, including a projection of future opportunities; third, an understanding of one's own abilities and potential vocational level, along with whatever training is possible to develop these abilities.

DEVELOPING INTELLECTUAL SKILLS AND CONCEPTS NECESSARY FOR CIVIC COMPETENCE

This and the next task are continuations and extensions of earlier tasks of conceptualization and skill development. It is one of the central tasks of the secondary school and is generated more by the necessities of society than by personal need. It is the one task of those listed in which the individual might fail and yet lead a happy and personally productive life. The concepts necessary for everyday living learned in the elementary school will suffice for the individual to get along in the world (17, p. 136; 17A, p. 54).

Contemporary American society requires the individual citizen to make many far reaching decisions based upon an understanding of government, law, politics, economics, international relations, geography, and the relationship of science to the modern world. It requires political action and civic participation. It requires enough persons willing to take civic leadership in order to implement decisions. Without the continuous achievement of this task, a democratic form of government, as we know it, cannot survive. The complexities of world problems demand that it be achieved at increasingly higher levels.

Unlike the other tasks, there are few direct immediate motivations for the adolescent in tackling this one. The way in which the school handles the area and relates it to other motivations is crucial to its accomplishment.

Although the school is the primary agent for this task, home and peer group contribute to the learning of civic competence. Discussions and conversations at home contribute both attitude and knowledge of citizenship related matters. Through the adolescent society, ways of organizing relationships among people are learned and skill in social techniques is developed. Membership in more formal clubs and organizations provides the laboratory setting for these learnings. Working together for a mutual cause or objective is an important skill earned in adolescence, which carries over into adult life and contributes to civic competence.

The adult society, represented by the school, and the adolescent society can come together in certain phases of extracurricular activities and student government to enhance the application of learnings in the social sciences to immediate concerns of adolescents. Many such bridges are necessary to accomplish this task through the adolescent years.

DESIRING AND ACHIEVING SOCIALLY RESPONSIBLE BEHAVIOR

Mastering the concepts and skills for civic competence has little function unless the individual wishes to use them and learns to use them in responsible social behavior. At the lowest acceptable level, this task implies general acceptance of societal controls on behavior, conformity to the general body of law, willingness and some ability to get along with others, and a personal behavior pattern that does not violate the values of society. At the highest level, it implies maximum participation in civic affairs on the neighborhood, community, or wider levels, with the tendency to accept leadership in such affairs. Personal behavior is consonant with the best values of the society and serves to enhance them. Obviously, the habitual juvenile delinquent or the withdrawn psychopath have failed in this task (17, p. 142; 17A, p. 57).

Most adolescents are not yet ready to perform at the highest level of achievement in this task. Adolescents can only meet the basic levels, engaging in socially responsible behavior within their own groups, and building attitudes toward future responsibility and leadership. Many young people, through concern for wider social issues and through leadership in their own groups are preparing for the achievement of adult civic and social responsibility.

In no other area of the developmental tasks is there as complex a shift of directions and change of required patterns as in the sequence of learning right and wrong, developing a conscience, and guiding behavior through an ethical system. Each stage seems to be necessary; however, at each stage, former patterns must be broken to permit the formation of the next stage. The literal commands and prohibitions of infancy are too simple and inadequate for the needs of childhood. Yet in childhood, the ego is not strong enough to handle moral and ethical issues without the help of a working conscience. The more subtly interpreted conscience and rudimentary scale of values developed during childhood prove inadequate for optimum fulfillment of the expanding horizon and greater impulse life of the adolescent. His increased tendency to think in terms of principles and abstract concepts permits the adolescent to deepen and expand his scale of values and to start building an ethical system, against which he can measure his conduct and that of others. As an adult, the healthy individual will still respond to the general direction of conscience and will be protected by guilt from flagrant violations. But his conduct will more adequately reflect moral judgments with finer discriminations based upon a more or less consistent ethical system. Increasingly, he will assess judgments as "correct or incorrect" as measured by their total effects, rather than as "right or wrong" in the more primitive absolute way of the child. The conscience is open to modification by reason (17, p. 147; 17A, p. 62).

At the highest level of accomplishment of this task, the individual will be making explicit a value system (emotionalized beliefs) and an ethical system (guide to behavior), which are consonant with a scientific world view. He will judge his behavior, and that of others, by its effects in as broad a context as possible. He will permit his emotions and impulse life to have joyous expression, controlled by perception of its consequences. Future goals are set at a level that requires striving but permits high probability of achievement. This may eventuate in a developing consistent personal philosophy of life.

There are a number of possibilities at the low or failure area for this task. They range from immoral or criminal values, which prevent adjustment to the larger society, to irrational conformity to a narrow set of given values. It is probable that the median accomplishment of this task in American society today results in conformity to the perceived expectations of one's own group.

Conformity to the values of the peer group is probably a necessary stage in the accomplishment of this task. However, a high level of accomplishment demands going beyond such an expedient to autonomous formulation of personal values and ethics.

SUMMARY OF THE DEVELOPMENTAL TASKS

The individual enters adolescence a child and leaves it a young adult. In the age span from twelve to twenty, nature and society demand tremendous transformations in the person. Some of these changes are made easy and others difficult in particular cultures. American cultures and subcultures provide a framework of pressures and opportunities, which tend to lead youth in certain directions. The developmental-task concept is one way of looking at this complex process.

It should be clear that in different societies, the precise nature of the developmental tasks will differ. Our society may be considered as a relatively open society, with a multivalued culture. There is more necessity and opportunity for decision making and more possibility for variation in successful mastery of the tasks. Interpretation of the nature of the society and desirable outcomes for individuals vary widely. It would be possible to describe the tasks at various levels of abstraction, stating one or more very general tasks for each level of development or listing hundreds of discrete tasks to be mastered in order to move ahead. The description used here chooses a medium level of abstraction that is, hopefully, helpful, stimulating to thought and application, but not overwhelming. The important consideration for psychology and education is the process of continuous psychological readjustment necessary in the progressive mastery of the tasks and its implications for teaching and learning.

Teachers and schools have many functions and desire many goals for their pupils. Very broadly and generally, many of these goals might be summed up in the notion of helping the learner become increasingly mature. What the teacher and the school mean by "maturity" becomes fundamental. Some analysis of the psychological use of the term may help to clarify possible meanings. Psychologically, maturity cannot be considered as an absolute or final state. One does not arrive at maturity and stay there. Rather, the term is used to designate a state of development relative to some external criterion. Thus, we can speak of an immature twelve-year-old, a mature twelve-year-old, or a very mature twelve-year-old. These designations are not precise; they indicate approximate positions on a scale of development, which expresses some notion of what twelve-year-oldness is or ought to be. Physical sexual maturity is a more definite concept susceptible of biological definition. In both cases, the concept of maturity implies readiness for the next stage, so that the immature twelve-year-old is considered unready to behave like the average twelve-year-old and is less ready than others to move on to thirteen-year-oldness.

MATURITY:
A GOAL
AND A GUIDE

13

When we fail to make a qualifying reference to maturity, we are likely to think of adulthood as the reference point. Yet, we can still talk about an immature adult. We probably implicitly use different criteria of maturity when using the term in reference to children and adults. During the developmental periods (conception to the end of adolescence, when maturation and learning are most rapid and change is highly visible), we tend to use the criterion of typical behavior for a given age level in assessing maturity. In adulthood (after adolescence, when change is less rapid and less visible), we tend to use some criterion based upon concepts of the proper and appropriate behavior of some ideal image. We further complicate the concepts by conceiving of a peak of maturity, which can deteriorate as in senility. With the very old, we speak of neither maturity nor immaturity, but of senility.

These apparent conflicts in conceptions of maturity can perhaps be resolved if we think of each stage of being as characterized by certain standards of behavior, derived from a comparison with typical behavior, the demands of readiness for the next stage, and some more distant goal toward which we expect movement. Thus, both the four-year-old becoming five and the forty-year-old becoming fifty are going through stages of development that can be assessed for maturity in the same way. It is possible that with increasing age, the more distant goal acquires increasing potency and conformity to typical behavior becomes less compelling.

The more distant stages of maturity become goals that must be taken into account in assessing maturity at any stage. For example, part of our estimate of the twelve-year-old's maturity depends upon our concept of the tasks and appropriate behavior of middle age and our judgment of whether he is moving on a path that will lead to the maturity of middle age. Readiness for the more proximate stage is more easily assessed, but that stage carries implications for the less proximate stages in the future.

This analysis of maturity has been implicit in the earlier discussion of psychosexual stages and developmental tasks. It is made explicit here as an introduction to the more mature levels of development and behavior. Such terms as "mental health," "adjustment," "normality," and "satisfaction of emotional needs" will come into the discussion of maturity as goals of development and guides to developmental stages.

DEVELOPMENTAL TASKS DURING THE ADULT YEARS

Development does not cease because one becomes adult. Continuous change, though of a different magnitude, is required to meet the responsibilities that come with early adulthood, middle age, and old age. Less research and study have gone into assessment of developmental tasks of these periods than those of earlier periods. The definition of tasks is less compelling, and one can find more exceptions to their necessity. But seeing these tasks as goals of maturity, it may be helpful to list them with a minimum of discussion as guide lines for referring backward and forward. The listing here follows Havighurst's treatment of the subject as did earlier statements of developmental tasks.

In meeting these tasks, the individual is more alone than at any other period. There are few institutions in society specifically geared to give him help. He must get what help he can by societal arrangements that incidentally impinge on his tasks. He must depend largely upon the maturity he brings with him from earlier periods. These are the tasks (17, pp. 259-76; 17A, pp. 72-82):

1. Selecting a mate.
2. Learning to live with a marriage partner.
3. Starting a family.
4. Rearing children.
5. Managing a home.
6. Getting started in an occupation.
7. Taking on civic responsibility.
8. Finding a congenial social group.

It will be noted that preparation for all of these tasks has been inherent in earlier tasks. Yet, the level of accomplishment demanded for personal happiness and for necessary contribution to society presents difficulties that give them a real task quality. These tasks also overlap with the tasks of infancy and early childhood of a new generation. For many young parents, there is a psychological re-enactment of their own childhood or at least a series of emotional responses that is triggered by the remnants in them of their own childhood.

DEVELOPMENTAL TASKS OF MIDDLE AGE

The time span of this period is not easily determined, but might be thought of as falling somewhere between ages thirty to fifty-five. These are the years in which, ideally, life reaches its peak of both personal fulfillment and social contribution. Thinking of maturity as a goal of growth, this is the period when most of the goals of maturity are potentially achievable. It is here that healthy development in earlier stages is expected to pay off. The developmental tasks are (17, pp. 268-76; 17A, pp. 83-91):

1. Achieving adult civic and social responsibility.
2. Establishing and maintaining an economic standard of living.
3. Assisting teenage children to become responsible and happy adults.
4. Developing adult leisure-time activities.
5. Relating oneself to one's spouse as a person.
6. Accepting and adjusting to the physiological changes of middle age.
7. Adjusting to aging parents.

Here again, there is the interlocking of developmental tasks for this age group with earlier and later generations. If teenage youngsters and their parents could see more clearly the tasks of each other, some conflicts might be reduced.

By the typical age of retirement, man's tasks are not yet over. In our society, adjustment to retirement, old age, and reduced vitality carries as many tasks as did infancy. The peak of development has passed, and the tasks become more personal (17, pp. 277-83; 17A, pp. 92-98).

1. Adjusting to decreasing physical strength and health.
2. Adjustment to retirement and reduced income.
3. Adjusting to death of spouse.
4. Establishing an explicit affiliation with one's age group.
5. Meeting social and civic obligations.
6. Establishing satisfactory physical living arrangements.

If maturity were a straight-line growth phenomenon, we might expect the years of old age to be the truly golden years. Actually, the above list has a curiously anticlimactic quality, which indicates that the growth process is truly running down. This period is beyond maturity in the goal-to-become-mature sense. Positive adjustment in old age depends upon the maturity one has achieved earlier. If one enters old age having reached the wisdom of psychological maturity, these tasks can be relatively easily achieved and the declining years can be a personally rewarding climax to long life. Yet the developmental-task concept gives little help as a way of setting final goals for the finishing years.

138

MATURITY AND PSYCHOSEXUAL DEVELOPMENT

Perhaps more useful in giving maturity a goal quality is the conception of psychosexual development, which has been analyzed in the preceding chapters from birth through adolescence. Less conformity-oriented than the developmental-task concept, this theory of development presents a specific model of desirable mature behavior as a goal of development toward which all earlier stages point.

The goal perceived by psychosexual developmental theory is an integrated personality, which shows a working balance of the phases described as id, ego, and superego (8, 9, 22). In its commerce with reality, the healthy ego deals with the developmental tasks and copes with the world productively at the highest possible level. In so doing, it finds acceptable outlets for id expression, so that feelings, emotions, and impulse life contribute to satisfaction in living and illuminate the behavior of the total person. At the same time, the superego serves its automatic control functions in such a way that it provides protection from thoroughly unacceptable impulses and acts without restricting constructive adjustments to the demands of the environment. The three phases of the personality become a cooperating system enhancing full functioning of the individual in constructive action in the world.

The outcome of such a process involves and permits empathy with others and a mutual relationship among people, which enriches the life of all concerned. This can be illustrated by the example of a mature love relationship, where the giving of oneself does not impoverish but enriches both the giver and receiver. Love, in this context, is not sacrifice of self, or even self-sacrifice; it is an expression of and an increment to the healthy integrative behavior of both partners. It is to this end that the shifting sexual focus of infancy, childhood, and adolescence has been leading. Oral, anal, and phallic pleasures were partially put aside in the service of ego and superego development. Genital pleasures were redeveloped and reorganized in the service of new id development and the integration of id, ego, and superego. It is not until the maturity of adulthood that the individual becomes a whole man in a whole world.

Less intense relationships among healthy people are similarly categorized by mutuality when the personality is adequate and balanced enough to deal with reality without needing to defend itself against the threat of insecurity. Nor does this concept of adequacy demand all gentleness and submission to others. Aggressiveness can be turned loose upon solving the real problems of the ego in dealing with the world and, at more contributing levels, upon solving some of the problems of the world.

There are many possibilities of different kinds of personalities within this concept of balance and integration as mature health. The reality experiences people have will result in varied interests and varied perceptions of reality. There is enough legitimate controversy in the world to keep life interesting for healthy individuals. The point is that external conflicts can be dealt with adequately only when internal conflicts are at a minimum.

Note also that this model, though stressing the importance of dealing objectively and rationally with the real world, does not divorce these activities from feelings. Reactions to the world are deep in feelings and emotions of all kinds precisely because the id phases of the personality and the revulsions of the superego are united with the ego-reality complex in an integrated action system.

In this interpretation of psychosexual development, we find a possible definition of maturity, which can serve as a goal and as a guide for assessing progress.

Like any model, this one is difficult of emulation. It is much easier to find adults who fail to achieve the goal of balanced personality integration than to find those who can be compared favorably with the model. This is not surprising when one considers the enormous complexity of the developmental process as it has been described. One of the potential values of psychological understanding is to enable individuals to work toward providing home, community, and school situations that will increasingly enhance movement toward this kind of maturity.

In old age, classical Freudian theory sees the dwindling of the life force and the increasing of the "death instinct," ending in the extinction of biologically based life (21). Contemporary interpretations of psychoanalysis make little use of this concept and actually have little to say about the final period of development. By extension, one would presume that the end product of healthy psychosexual development would be a period of personal happiness within the framework of acceptance of reality.

Three other terms need to be analyzed to clarify the goal of maturity and to distinguish between psychological conceptions of that goal and the everyday language of the layman. The terms "mental health," "adjustment," and "normal" have much in common with the concept of maturity discussed above.

The mentally healthy person has been characterized as a person who can meet, face, and take what comes. He also has the tendency to do something positive about it. This is not unlike the description of the healthy ego as one that copes constructively with reality. By implication, mental health introduces another dimension, its opposite side, ill health or mental illness. Just as a fortunate combination of circumstances playing upon the forces of development can produce a mature or a healthy person, so unfortunate circumstances at inappropriate times can produce mental illness or pathological immaturity. The health metaphor has also come to imply that adequacy of personality exists in degrees—that one is more or less healthy or unhealthy, rather than completely sick or completely well. There is the further analogy that a therapeutic environment can be used to improve one's health (22).

"Adjustment" seems to have become an emotionally tainted word to many critics of contemporary mental health theory. It is often equated with "conformity." Actually, the word is used in a number of ways, some more acceptable to psychological theory than others.

There are, of course, many ways of adjusting. Conforming to the demands of others is one, but only one, of these ways. Some mental health theorists would contend that adjustment is a neutral word to describe a universal process and that all behavior can be talked about as some kind of adjustment of the total organism-environment complex. In this sense, the student, the teacher, the criminal, and the doctor and his patient in the mental hospital are all examples of particular kinds of adjustment to the pressures brought to bear upon them. In this same sense, it can be said that each person makes the best adjustment he can, given his particular life history and life space.

When used more technically with a specific designator of degree of adjustment, as in "well adjusted" or "maladjusted," the term is almost synonymous with the conception of integration or maturity of psychosexual adjustment. The person who is well adjusted has a minimum of internal conflicts and is free to deal realistically with the world. The person who is maladjusted is, to some extent, dominated by internal conflicts and is less able to turn his energy outward. Either person may or may not "conform"; the important thing is the motivation or impulsion behind the conformity or lack of it.

With another specific modifier, *social* adjustment implies some degree of conformity to social customs and the amenities that lubricate social intercourse. Psychologically, this is only one characteristic; it may or may not be important in a particular individual's total adjustment.

"Normal" is another ambiguous word when used in the field of personality dynamics. At least three distinct meanings can be distinguished.

First, the most defensible meaning is the one derived from statistics. The normal person is the one who falls within the limits of a central tendency measure on a frequency curve of the occurrence of a particular characteristic among a given population or an adequate sample of that population. For example, if we had an adequate measure of mental health or personality integration so that the measures could be arranged from low to high, those persons who scored amound the middle of the curve, the average, would be normal. It is difficult to find and apply an adequate measure of this kind to an adequate sample. If we were to do so, it is probable that the "normal" individual in contemporary American society would be somewhat "maladjusted" or neurotic.

The other two uses of the word are quite different from this technical use, but are closely related to each other. "Normal" is frequently used to refer to a person who is free of symptoms of ill health. He is, thus, phenotypically mentally healthy. The other allied use of the term refers to appropriate positive behavior or to deeper motivations in the personality as when we say, "his reactions were normal," meaning that he gave the expected response to a particular situation. Used this way, the term frequently implies a rather high level of personality integration.

This terminology has been explored at some length, because personality and the behavior stemming from it are among the main concerns of teachers and schools. Clarity of concepts in this area and a language with which to communicate them may be helpful in organizing reality so that it may be dealt with.

141

PERSONALITY NEEDS AND BEHAVIOR

At adult stages as well as during the developmental periods, the personality needs of the individual are among the funadmental motivations of behavior. The more immature the individual, the more this is so. The infant is almost wholly controlled by his unmet needs. The mature personality is relatively able to respond to the objective world, because needs have been met at a relatively high level. Rational analysis and effective decision-making depend upon a high level of personality integration, in which unmet needs are at a minimum. Where there is conflict within the personality, behavior is more likely to reflect the conflict than to deal with objective reality.

A very popular psychological theory in regard to needs and behavior has been referred to as the frustration-aggression hypothesis (7). This hypothesis states that when a person is frustrated in his wishes or desires, the most likely response is aggressive behavior. That is, he will fight back against the perceived frustrator. It is obvious that the term frustration is here reserved for reactions beyond mere temporary lack of satisfaction or temporary failure to solve a problem. While a problem is perceived as possible of solution, the individual may tackle it in many ways. He may analyze it carefully and apply a number of potential alternative solutions until it is solved. Fighting back may be one of these appropriate solutions. Frustration refers to blockings of desire where realistic solutions are not perceived, where satisfaction is not anticipated. It is here that unrealistic aggression becomes the typical mode of response. To define this hypothesis in detail would require a rather elaborate discussion, involving highly sophisticated psychological ideas. For example, some people obviously withdraw or escape from the frustration situation. How can this be defined as aggression? By invoking a number of psychological mechanisms, it could be demonstrated that such behaviors are a displaced form of aggression. For our purpose, it may be simpler and just as satisfactory to say that frustration results in behavior that is maladaptive in a reality situation. That is, the behavior may make the frustration temporarily less painful, but fails to solve the problem in the long run and also fails to lead to more mature adaptations.

By extension, this same hypothesis can be applied to the frustration of needs at any level of development. Frustration of needs at the anal level will result in immediate maladaptive behavior and make it difficult to move on to the phallic level. Frustration of adolescent needs will cause maladaptive behavior (withdrawal, violent rebellion, antisocial acts) and make it more difficult to become a well-functioning adult. Obversely, satisfaction of needs at any level will result in more appropriate immediate behavior and will permit movement to the next stage of maturity.

It would logically follow that the person whose needs are severely and consistently frustrated will continue to show characteristics of immaturity, will be less able to deal constructively with reality, and will be more vulnerable to later threats of frustration. The person who has consistently had his needs met will be better able to resist the threat of frustration—his "frustration tolerance" will be higher.

Does this mean that *all* needs should be *immediately* satisfied in order to develop mature adjustment? It would be interesting to speculate on such a possibility, but it is scarcely a viable question. The distinction is between frustration as defined above and delayed satisfaction. Frustration connotes the blocking of potential satisfaction in such a way that the need remains unmet. The individual, consciously or unconsciously, expects it to be unmet and fails to find ways for satisfactorily meeting it. This is the harmful level.

On the other hand, for a need to have any potency or significance for motivation or development it must exist, and existence implies some duration of time. Only by the most unrealistic abstraction can we talk about the need for nourishment if the baby constantly receives proper nutrients by intravenous feeding. The hunger need becomes real when there is enough delay in feeding so that the body is temporarily deprived of nutrients long enough to require replenishment. The hunger need becomes potent for behavior when the baby engages in some activity likely to help satisfy the need. A need for affection can not develop if the baby is constantly smothered with attention. More likely he will develop a need to be left alone!

The constructive level of need functioning requires enough time for deprivation to develop the need, sufficient duration of the need to make it potent, and satisfaction of the need. The ways in which satisfaction is obtained will eventually determine typical modes of mature behavior.

It may be helpful to think of needs as functioning on three possible levels: the developmental level, the frustration level, and the maintenance level. The developmental level refers to the operation of needs at the time they become potent, when their satisfaction makes possible the movement to the next stage of growth. Thus, in the anal period, the anal needs become potent for establishing the behavior and personality characteristics associated with that period. If they are satisfied during that period, the individual is free to move on to the phallic stage and meet the needs characteristic of that period.

If the anal needs develop and are not satisfied during the anal period, they are frustrated and are carried at the frustration level into the next period, where they interfere with continued normal development.

If the anal needs are satisfied at the developmental level during the appropriate developmental period, they are not eliminated. They still exist at the maintenance level. The behaviors associated with them continue in mature behavior, and the individual continues to satisfy these needs without problems or anxieties concerning them. If circumstances in maturity should give the anal needs new potency, the individual can handle them realistically and find ways to reduce any harmful effects.

This same classification can be applied to needs at all levels so that we might diagnose maturity of behavior in terms of the degree to which needs have been satisfied at developmental levels.

Thus, specific behavior of individuals, whether children or adults, is partially dictated by the needs structure of the person and the dynamic interactions within this structure. As teachers try to understand their own behavior and the behavior of learners, a needs theory may provide one set of keys for doing so. As teachers help children develop and change their behavior, a needs theory can be helpful in providing the basis for diagnosis and treatment.

SPECIFIC NEEDS THEORIES AND THEIR IMPLICATIONS FOR BEHAVIOR

In Chapter 7, several specific needs theories were discussed as they related to learning theory. The Maslovian concepts will be re-examined here as an intriguing example of guide lines toward maturity.

It will be recalled that Maslow conceives of a hierarchy of needs, operating in such a way that higher-level needs emerge as lower-level needs are routinely satisfied. Maturity might be defined as consisting of behavior motivated increasingly by higher-level needs. The person operating primarily at the physiological or safety level would be relatively immature, while one operating largely at the self-actualizing level would be relatively mature.

To recapitulate the needs as described in Chapter 7, but to put them now in developmental order, they are (19):

1. Physiological needs
2. Safety needs
3. Love and belonging needs
4. Esteem needs
5. Self-actualization needs

This list may be considered hierarchical in two senses: first, it parallels development in a temporal sense; second, it progresses toward maturity and health in a value sense.

In the temporal sense, there can be a rough equation of dominance by these needs with the various developmental stages. The neonate is largely dominated by the physiological needs. Safety and love needs develop from the physiological needs and are dominant throughout childhood. Esteem needs, which seem to be generally characteristic of adolescents, change their character in early adulthood to motivate achievement and the establishment of adult activities. Consistent self-actualizing can scarcely occur until the tasks of early adulthood are met.

However, this temporal hierarchy should not be taken too seriously. All five needs levels may show themselves as operational at any developmental stage. The school-age child is occasionally dominated by physiological needs. Much of his intellectual activity is devoted to creating an orderly and predictable world, in which he can be assured a modicum of psychological safety. In his activities with same sex play groups, he seeks love and belonging. Temporarily assured of this, he may seek to assert leadership or to exhibit spectacular achievement to go beyond love to gain the esteem of his fellows—thus, acquiring the self-esteen that makes self-actualizing possible. There will be times in play or in intellectual exploration when he goes beyond the lower-level needs and engages in an activity just because it is right for him.

The same web of motivation, though in different proportions, may be characteristic of an individual in early childhood or adolescence. At any level of development, we may anticipate a particular kind of web, but we may assess the maturity of the individual by the frequency of higher-level motivations.

Progression in a value sense is implicit in the above discussion. It may, however, need illustration. Let us take two apparently disparate activities to serve as examples: sexual activity of an adult and school achievement activities in a child.

Sexual activity is selected as an example because it is obviously central to the psychosexual development concept. There is also a tendency to think of it as responsive primarily to the love needs. This is not necessarily so.

For some people, sexual gratification whether obtained through intercourse or otherwise is almost entirely on the physiological level. Release of physiological tension is all that is desired and all that is obtained. Others are blocked in even achieving this release because of highly powerful but distorted safety needs. Others are fixated in a particular kind of sexual activity because it is unsafe to move on to the development of love needs. A person motivated at the love-need level may develop a true love object to whom he gives affection and from whom he receives affection. Physical love is either an expression or a token of that affection. Yet, if this need remains unsatisfied, the individual keeps seeking ways to satisfy it; he cannot respond to the esteem of the loved one or develop self-esteem unless the need is satisfied. There are those who use sexual activity as they would an achievement, seeking admiration or esteem for their prowess. Only at the self-actualizing level is sexual activity incorporated into creative self-expression, which is capable of desiring and achieving mutuality without being driven by lower-level needs.

Study activities leading to academic achievement in school may be motivated similarly at various levels. The physiological needs are positive motivation only under extremely rare conditions. Perhaps some cases of the "brain washing" of prisoners during the Korean War might be interpreted as academic type learning under forced physiological deprivation. Even here, probably, safety needs were more the motivator. Usually, the physiological-need level serves to interfere with the mastery of academic material, though a person deeply involved in study from a higher motivational level may seriously violate his physiological needs to some degree.

More typically, motivation for academic activity comes from the safety level or above, with different implications for quality of learning. Motivation at the safety level may have two phases: activity to avoid physical harm or the threat thereof and the attempt to find psychological safety by learning to make the world an orderly and predictable place. Love and belonging are motivations when the child identifies with parents and teachers and orders his activity to demonstrate and receive love. Similarly, activities designed to imitate and to make one acceptable to one's peers are on the same level. It is clear that these motives, under certain circumstances, may impede as well as enhance a high level of learning.

When the individual becomes autonomous enough to respond to the respect and esteem of others, he may engage in academic learning when he perceives this as valued by significant others. Being esteemed for scholarship motivates much academic activity, especially of the formal kind. As the individual's self-concept grows—as he perceives himself a scholar—self-esteem motivates relatively independent activity.

On occasions when the study activity becomes intrinsically satisfying or when the topics or ideas under consideration become valued for their own sake, academic learning is motivated by self-actualization needs. This level is probably characteristic of creative thinkers at the mature level and of some problem solving and discovery activities throughout childhood.

There might be a suggestion here for teachers to search for and enhance the kinds of learning activities that can be responded to in a self-actualizing mode.

Many people are finding the Maslovian schema an extremely fruitful way of conceiving guides to maturity.

RATHS' CONCEPT OF EMOTIONAL NEEDS

Another theory of emotional needs as behavioral motivation has been developed and applied by Louis Raths and his students (24). This system may be considered as having less theoretical power than Maslow's concepts; however, it has more immediate application for diagnosis and treatment of children. Designed to help teachers better understand the emotional needs of children and to improve their dealings with them, this system has demonstrated its usefulness in practice.

Like other needs approaches, this theory hypothesizes that satisfaction of needs leads to balanced-objective-productive behavior and freedom to operate on higher levels, resulting in an expanding self. On the other hand, long-range or immediate frustration of needs leads to less appropriate behavior, which is eventually self-defeating, resulting in a restriction of self. Expanding the frustration-aggression hypothesis, Raths defines four kinds of symptomatic behaviors. They are aggression, submission, withdrawal, and psychosomatic illness. Without restricting inappropriate behavior to these four types, it is suggested that the bulk of such behavior can be so classified. When such behavior exists at a problem level, diagnosis of need frustration can be followed by attempts to satisfy the needs, resulting in a reduction of inappropriate activities and a more positive behavioral response.

Raths does not stress the hierarchical nature of needs but rather suggests that we are all motivated by a pattern of needs in varying degrees of satisfaction and frustration. It is this pattern that produces characteristic behavior. A shift in the level of satisfaction of the pattern of needs will result in an equivalent behavioral shift. Raths' discussion of needs does not group them in categories or in hierarchical order. They are here listed in categories that direct attention to the similarities between this list and our previous discussion. The list is short enough to be kept in mind for practical use:

> *Dependence needs*
> To be loved
> To belong
> To feel economically secure
>
> *Independence needs*
> To understand
> To achieve
>
> *Intrapersonal needs*
> To be free of excessive guilt feelings
> To be free of excessive fears
>
> *Maturity needs*
> To share and have self-respect

The first three needs emphasize dependence on others, and their satisfaction gives feelings of security. To be loved implies acceptance with no strings attached. The child needs to feel that he is loved just because he exists without reference to his achievement or conformity behaviors. To belong implies group membership and, at higher levels, participation in movements or belief systems that relate one to others. To feel economically secure is only partly an objective condition. It also carries the implication of not being too different in economic condition from others about you. Beyond the physiological needs and subsistence level, it is partly an acceptance of status.

The independence needs imply the need to act upon the world—to understand and make sense out of things, people, and relationships—and to accomplish or achieve in that world.

A look at these five needs permits discussion of the importance of diagnosis and differential satisfaction. If a child (or an adult) is frustrated in

his need to achieve, giving him love will not solve the problem—he needs help in achieving. If the frustrated need is belonging, understanding why he does not belong may eventually lead to improvement; it does not directly remove the frustration. Of course, in the case of seriously disturbed children, a whole series of needs are frustrated; and help in almost any area can be valuable.

It should also be apparent at this point that a need cannot be oversatisfied. Technically, a child cannot, for example, be given "too much love." The child who is "smothered with love" should be perceived as frustrated in the independence needs—kept from understanding and achieving. The excessive love is not oversatisfying the first need, it is frustrating the fourth and fifth. In treatment, the correct approach is not withdrawal of love as such, but opportunity and encouragement to achieve.

The intrapersonal needs are referred to the personality dynamics and internal conflicts that can interfere with healthy objective behavior. Excessive guilt feelings restrict behavior in the world and militate against personal happiness. Caution and reasonable safety require some degree of fear of actually harmful things; however, the person with excessive fears is blocked in normal activity.

Finally, the need to share and have self-respect is an interesting two-sided coin. It implies that one can respect oneself only as he can share of himself. One must alternately respect self enough to feel that the sharing makes a contribution and to learn that the contribution further enhances self-respect. It is not necessarily better to give than to receive; one receives by giving.

These eight needs are seen as psychological with a strong emotional tone. They are deeply felt, and the balance of satisfaction and frustration among them impels both overt responses to situations and the characteristic quality of an individual's behavior.

The four types of deviant behavior classified as responses to frustration are aggression, submission, withdrawal, and psychosomatic illness.

Aggressive behavior is appropriate when it is directed at the solution of real problems and when it is an assertion of principles basic to the integrity of self. Frustration motivated aggression is more likely to seem pointless to the outside observer. Children (or adults) who swear, hit, fight, destroy, and deliberately oppose others for no apparent reason are acting aggressively in ways that may be symptomatic of unmet needs. Such behaviors are likely to be met by counter-aggression from others (since such behavior tends to frustrate the needs of others), and the results are unproductive of genuine solution of the frustrating condition.

Similarly, the frustrated individual may fail to fight back and may compromise with the frustration by submitting, by giving in, by doing what others tell him, and by taking no responsibility for independent action. This may seem safer than striking out. Frequently, teachers and other adults fail to see submissive behavior as symptomatic of emotional distress, because the submissive child does what he is told unless personal initiative is required.

Other people may react to frustration by withdrawing from frustrating situations. Because this does not permit any activity to overcome the frustration, it becomes more and more self-defeating. Ultimately, contact with reality can become more and more tenuous and any productive activity less likely.

Still other people literally make themselves sick with their conflicts. Symptoms of illness that are emotionally inspired may have the secondary advantage of permitting withdrawal with social approval. From asthma to ulcers, there are many documentations of illnesses primarily related to emotional frustrations.

Obviously, all of us act in these four ways at various times. Temporary frustration of needs unbalances our behavior. However, if the frustration is of long standing or is persistent, the deviant behavior will also be more characteristic and persistent.

There is considerable evidence that when teachers and others are aware of these needs and take steps to help children meet them, deviant behavior is reduced (24). Because we all have these needs, at least at a maintenance level, situations that tend to satisfy them result in more appropriate behavior. If teachers provide situations where children know they are loved and accepted, where they are encouraged to belong in the group, where understanding and achievement are made possible and desirable, where children are minimally threatened by punishment, and where sharing and respect are built into personal relationships, total behavior will tend to be positive.

If teachers can learn to go beyond providing this help for children who have unmet needs at a serious level—taking special care to provide satisfying situations in line with individual diagnosis—positive improvements in mental health and behavior will occur, including improvement in the learning of concepts, attitudes, and skills.

EMOTIONAL PROBLEMS AND THE TEACHER

As teachers, we satisfy the needs of learners not for the sake of satisfaction, but to help them move on to a more advanced stage of development. We engage in mental health practices, not only because they are good in themselves, but because they make possible the achievement of the positive aims of the school, the society, and the individual himself. Interferences in development within the normal range must be alleviated by the teacher in order for optimum learning to take place.

What is the teacher's responsibility when serious interferences have occurred in normal development, so that the child is seriously disturbed or engages in behavior so deviant that it is considered beyond the normal range? In the first place, it must be recognized that teachers, as products of their own development and motivated by their own needs structures, will vary in their ability to tolerate deviant behavior. Hence, one teacher may be able to go considerably beyond another in coping with what he considers excessive deviance. Teachers will vary in the amount of insight they have into particular behavior problems. Their interest, training, and ability to deal with personality problems will also vary.

Given these variables, effective teachers must understand themselves and their own motivations well enough to control their own behavior in dealing with the immature. They must then understand the motivations and behavior patterns of their students well enough to recognize deviations that they can or cannot handle. Finally, they should know enough about deviations that are beyond their treatment potential to get help or make appropriate referrals to persons or agencies who have the necessary skills. These principles apply to serious learning difficulties, as well as to clear emotional difficulties.

It is beyond the scope of this volume to give training in therapy or a working understanding of neuroses, psychoses, or modes of treatment. Far beyond the foundations of education are the professional skills a teacher must develop in helping all children grow to maturity. If prospective teachers can gain a basic understanding of the forces at work in development, it is hoped they will be impelled to seek detailed understandings and to develop the techniques necessary for effective guidance toward the goals of maturity.

As one grows and develops, one phase of development, namely, intelligence, is of particular interest to teachers and of particular importance for schooling.

WHAT IS INTELLIGENCE?

Intelligence is the name given to a certain class of behavior, or more abstractly, to the quality of a certain class of behavior. We say that a person has a certain level of intelligence or does things "intelligently." The behaviors are subsumed under such terms as perceiving, remembering, seeing relationships, comprehending, abstracting, applying principles to concrete situations, manipulating ideas, and expressing ideas. The qualities of these activities are expressed by such notions as speed in performing these operations, the intricacy or richness of associations, and the correctness of outcomes of these activities. The degree to which these behaviors are successfully performed is represented by such words as brilliant, bright, smart, dull, dumb, or stupid. We say that a highly intelligent person "catches on" quickly or that a less intelligent one "never sees the point." We sometimes talk as though intelligence were a unitary quality—as though one were

INTELLIGENCE:
A PHASE
OF DEVELOPMENT

14

either bright or dull in all situations. This is obviously not true. Each of us can find some situations in which we can "catch on" quickly and others in which we cannot react intelligently. Yet, if we look at a broad spectrum of behavior, there is a characteristic quality of response or there is at least a possible average of our responses, which makes it possible to talk about a characteristic level of intelligence.

Intelligence, then, is not a "thing." It is a label given to certain characteristics of behavior and then referred to the person who exhibits this behavior as a relatively stable characteristic of his personality. It is only one phase of the personality and not necessarily descriptive of the total person. Yet, it is an important phase in assessing the individual's ability to adapt to life situations, especially situations involving tasks traditionally associated with education and schooling.

It is useful to think of intelligence as the ability to profit from experience or to modify behavior as a result of experiencing. As we have earlier defined learning, intelligence may be thought of as the ability to learn, describable in terms of degrees of that ability.

ASSESSING AND DESCRIBING INTELLIGENCE

People have long had global notions about intelligence. One of the major achievements of psychology is that it has found ways to talk about intelligence more precisely and to organize our understanding of it so that communication is possible.

The main line of psychological thinking about intelligence and its assessment may be traced to the work of Alfred Binet in France around the turn of the century. Faced with a request from the Ministry of Public Instruction to develop a test for the early identification of mentally defective children, Binet and his collaborators used a minimum of systematic theory and sought empirical evidence of children's behaviors that might be considered intelligent. Using a series of questions and relatively simple performance tasks, they started to identify tasks that could be performed, or problems that could be solved, by typical children of a particular age level. Working by hunches and successive approximations, they found a limited series of tasks that would differentiate the performance of average children year by year. For example, eight-year-olds who could not do tasks beyond those usually mastered by the average six-year-old were obviously below average. On the other hand, eight-year-olds who could perform the tasks at a level characteristic of average ten-year-olds were well above average.

Binet and Simon published scales of tests, graded according to age of typical performance, in 1905, 1908, and 1911. The final version contained a limited number of tasks or "tests" for age levels from three to sixteen, with indications for a level of performance characteristic of each age. It is interesting that this approach uses a "developmental" concept as outlined in preceding chapters, even though, at that time, there was little developmental theory and there were few empirical studies of the actual behavioral development of children. The term "mental age" refers to this concept, in that the child who performed on these tests like a typical ten-year-old was said to have a mental age of ten, regardless of his chronological age.

The terms "slow" and "fast," which have since become common in discussions of intelligence, thus, refer primarily to the pace of development and only secondarily to actual speed in performance or quickness of response.

The practical significance of Binet's work for American psychology and education lies in the fact that his scale was revised and adapted for American use by Terman at Stanford University in 1916. The Stanford revision of the Binet-Simon scale (usually referred to as the Stanford-Binet scale) has become the reference point for most work in the assessment and measurement of intelligence. Even theories that disagree with the implications of this scale must use it as a basis for discussion. The 1916 scale was revised in 1937 and again in 1960. The bulk of literature and discussion in recent years (up to 1964) has been based on the 1937 revision (29).

The kinds of tasks used to assess intelligence at various age levels vary from identifying objects by name, building a tower of blocks, and obeying simple commands at the earliest levels through recognizing an increasingly complex vocabulary, identifying similarities of objects, repeating a series of digits, and identifying incongruities or absurdities in pictures at the middle levels to using advanced vocabulary, dealing with abstract reasoning problems, and achieving higher levels of various performances at the advanced levels. Typically, there are six tasks for each given level on the Stanford-Binet test.

152   Note that there are no a priori theories involved in the construction and use of these scales. They are based upon trials with children until a standard of performance is reached that can be said to be typical of the average at each particular level and, thus, can be said to give a performance description of a particular mental age.

When Binet's original assignment to identify children who need special class help is compared to the empirical approach he developed, an interesting implicit assumption is revealed. *If children have been slow (or fast) in developing up to this time, they will probably continue at a similar pace.* Thus, the test score is seen not only as a description of present behavior, but as a statement about past development and as a prediction of continuing future development.

This assumption was made explicit in the development of the idea of the intelligence quotient, which compared mental age to chronological age as a ratio between performance and the length of time the individual had lived. With the intelligence quotient (or IQ), we can determine a child's mental age and we can also determine the ratio between his mental and chronological age. A child whose mental and chronological age are both ten has an IQ ratio of 10 to 10 or 1 to 1. A child with a mental age of ten (performing on the test items like an average ten-year-old) may be eight years old chronologically. He is younger than his performance would indicate, and his IQ ratio is 10 to 8. Another child may score at a mental age of ten, but may have been living for twelve years. His ratio would be 10 to 12.

The notion of this relationship between mental age and chronological age was developed for convenience into a single numerical statement without fractions or decimals by expressing the ratio as $\frac{MA}{CA} \times 100$, where MA means mental age as determined by performance on a standardized test, CA means chronological age in terms of years or months since birth, and 100 is a constant used to remove fractions or decimals. Thus, the preceding three examples would be described as having IQ's of 100, 125, and 83 respectively. The younger child with the higher mental age will have the higher IQ.

Since the Binet type test was developed empirically as a description of typical behavior at various age levels, we might assume that this is all it is. There is no logical reason to assume that a child who has an IQ of 100 at age 10 will again have an IQ of 100 if measured at age 12. Each testing might be idiosyncratic and give results independent of every other testing; however, an assumption of the constancy of the IQ has usually been made. To some degree, empirical studies have shown this assumption of relative constancy to be correct. Exceptions to this general statement will be analyzed later.

Out of this assumption and the evidence supporting it has come the conception of the intelligence quotient as a statement of *rate of growth* of intelligence. Putting this as a statement related to our definition of intelligence as the ability to profit from experience, if we take age level as the basis for assessing experience, we may assume that children who have been living for the same period of time have been exposed to essentially similar experiences. If their behavior differs, we may assume that they have benefited differentially from the experience. Their behavior level at any particular age will reflect the rate at which they have developed and is taken as a prediction of future behavior at a similar rate of development.

There is no necessary implication at this point that this is a genetic or "natural" difference. This question will be raised later. The examples given here simply spell out the assumptions and the general findings involved in Binet type testing and the IQ concept.

Applications of intelligence testing. Let us extend a hypothetical example to indicate the process of testing and prediction, as well as some of its implications for teaching.

Assume that we have a highly favored school system, in which individual intelligence testing is done as a regular routine (a situation that would be very difficult to find in practice). Let us further assume that each child is given a Stanford-Binet test upon entrance to kindergarten, and let us look at three children who might enter this school. Let us say that each of these children, whom we will call Alma, Ben, and Carol, is exactly five years old chronologically when tested.

Alma performs as follows on the test (29): Year IV tests are all passed and scored plus. Because this is the highest level at which Alma passes all tests, it is called the basal year and is credited at 4 years. Prior to Year V in the Stanford-Binet tests, there are a set of six tests for each half year. The examiner continues with the Year IV-6 tests, and Alma passes four of these, scored as 4 months. In the Year V set (covering Year IV-6 to Year V) Alma passes four tests and is scored at 4 months. She passes four of the Year VI tests (now six tests for the entire year), scoring 8 months. At Year VII she passes three tests for a score of 6 months and reaches her limit in Year VIII where she passes one test for 2 months credit. Further checking indicates that later tests are beyond her. To summarize Alma's record:

	Years	Months
Year IV, all plus. Basal year level	4	
Year IV-6, 4 tests passed, credit 1 month each		4
Year V, 4 tests passed, credit 1 month each		4
Year VI, 4 tests passed, credit 2 months each		8
Year VII, 3 tests passed, credit 2 months each		6
Year VIII, 1 test passed, credit 2 months		2
	4	24 or
Mental age score	6	0

Alma's mental age is computed as six years. It will be noted that this score is based upon a range of performance from below her age level to well above it, including passing at least one test that is designed for eight-year-olds. According to this record, Alma has achieved six years of intellectual growth in five years of living. Her growth rate has been 1.2 mental years per chronological year.

Ben's performance may be summed up as follows:

	Years	Months
Year III-6, all plus. Basal year level	3	6
Year IV, 5 tests passed, credit 1 month each		5
Year IV-6, 3 tests passed, credit 1 month each		3
Year V, 4 tests passed, credit 1 month each		4
Year VI, 2 tests passed, credit 2 months each		4
Year VII, 1 test passed, credit 2 months each		2
	3	24 or
Mental age score	5	0

Ben is credited with a mental age of five years, the same as his chronological age. It is possible that, even though scoring lower than Alma, Ben may have passed some individual tests that Alma couldn't pass. Specific performances might be quite different, Ben doing better on certain kinds of tasks, Alma on others. Ben's growth has been five years in five years of living or a growth rate of one year per year.

Carol's record might look like the following:

	Years	Months
Year III, all plus. Basal year level	3	
Year III-6, 4 tests passed, credit 1 month each		4
Year IV, 3 tests passed, credit 1 month each		3
Year IV-6, 2 tests passed, credit 1 month each		2
Year V, 1 test passed, credit 1 month		1
Year VI, 1 test passed, credit 2 months		2
	3	12 or
Mental age score	4	0

Carol is credited with a mental age of four years, even though she passes at least one test at the six-year-old level. Her growth rate has been .8 of a mental year per chronological year; she has accomplished four years of progress in five years of living.

Let us assume that the testing is accurate and that development proceeds according to usual predictions. Let us further assume that this school system generally moves children through school on an age-level basis, so that Alma, Ben, and Carol go through school together. Projecting their development, we would predict the following:

Age	5	6	7	8	9	10	11	12	13	14	15	16	17	18
Grade	K	1	2	3	4	5	6	7	8	9	10	11	12	

Mental Age

Alma	6	7.2	8.4	9.6	10.8	12	13.2	14.4	15.6	16.8	18	19.2	20.4	21.6
Ben	5	6.0	7.0	8.0	9.0	10	11.0	12.0	13.0	14.0	15	16.0	17.0	18.0
Carol	4	4.8	5.6	6.4	7.2	8	8.8	9.6	10.4	11.2	12	12.8	13.6	14.4

To the extent that accomplishment in scholastic work follows mental age, we would expect great differences in the performance of these three children. In general, other things being equal, academic skills such as reading, writing, and computation tend to follow mental age rather closely. Information-getting is less directly related; however, under appropriate stimulation, it also tends to follow mental age. Ignoring the other variables for the time being, Ben should be capable of working at grade level throughout his school career. Alma may be stimulated to work above grade level, but she is able to work at grade level without exerting herself. By the time the children enter seventh grade, Alma should be capable of reading with a ninth-grade or fourteen-year-old level of skill. At the same time, Carol will be doing well if she is proficient with fourth-grade level material.

The gap in mental age increases year by year. The two-year difference between Alma and Carol in kindergarten becomes a four-year difference by grade five, and a six-year difference by grade ten. By the time they finish high school, they will be seven years apart in probable intellectual development. Teaching these three children and their classmates will require great variation in content, methods, and materials if effective learning is to take place.

It is beyond the scope of this discussion to indicate the possible varieties of school organization and instructional differentiation that have been designed to care for these developmental differences. They vary from ungraded schools to grade-skipping and retention, from individualized instruction to so-called homogeneous grouping, from specialized materials to common standards. Psychologically, the fact remains that some provision must be made for these intellectual differences if effective learning is to be permitted for all children.

The terminology of the intelligence quotient has been avoided in the discussion of Alma, Ben, and Carol, because the significant practical concept lies in the mental age. We are likely to think of IQ as an absolute measure of brightness, although its major significance is as a simple statement of growth rate, the relatively constant relationship between mental age and chronological age. With attention focussed on mental age, it is obvious that Alma has an IQ of 120, Ben 100, and Carol 80. This relationship remains constant in the above examples, indicating the increments of growth year by year as 1.2, 1, and .8 respectively.

In any comprehensive school, children in the same grade level may have an IQ range of from 75 or below to 140 or above; in mental age, there may be differences of from four to twelve years.

Other Implications of the IQ. Although the IQ is technically a statement of the growth rate, it does have other meanings. Alma will be perceived as "brighter" than Carol. She will be intellectually more alert. Adults will probably see her as more mature. Her perceptions of reality will be more in accord with those of adults, and she will more readily see relationships among the facets of living. She will be able to take into account more aspects of life in problem-solving activities. In effect, there will be a qualitative difference as well as a quantitative difference in her intellectual grasp of the world around her. As an adult, she will handle language more accurately and more fluently, and will be more likely to display evidence of intellectual curiosity.

In other facets of development, there is no guarantee that the more intelligent will be more advanced than the less intelligent. Physical growth and maturity seems to be relatively independent of intelligence, correlating more highly with body type than with IQ as such. Emotional balance and social maturity have some relation to intelligence, but many other factors seem to affect them more. In the early years, gross motor skills have some relation to developing intelligence, but many highly intelligent adults do not display advanced motor skills to any greater degree than the less intelligent. Wide variations in intelligence, as in the genius and the mentally deficient, show greater differences in other factors than one finds within the normal range.

On the other hand, there is considerable evidence that "positive" factors in development tend to go together in some slight degree (28, 30, pp. 424-35). Measures of height, weight, social adjustment, and physical and emotional health correlate positively with intelligence. The popular conception of the genius as inferior in appearance and adjustment is not upheld by research. The mentally inferior individual is more likely to be inferior in other ways while the mentally superior individual tends to be generally superior. These relationships are generally true, but are not sufficiently strong for individual prediction. Any single person who is of superior intelligence may or may not be superior in other ways. Intelligence, as defined, is one phase of development. To the extent that various phases are correlated, it will give a clue to total development; however, it gives no sure key to the total individual.

THE CONTINUANCE AND CESSATION OF MENTAL GROWTH

The development of theory and research on intelligence has been largely developmental. That is, we know more about the growth of intelligence through the developmental years than we know about adult intelligence.

It is clear that those who are mentally superior tend to maintain their superiority in adult life, but adult adjustment of the less intellectually able is less clear. We have probably all had the common-sense experience of knowing people who were correctly considered dull or stupid in school and of finding them years later to be quite adequate, though not superior, adults. It seems as though maturity has enabled them to "catch up" to the average. Though profiting less in the year by year schedule of development, the years of maturity have enabled them to profit enough to get along. There are few adequate psychological studies of this phenomenon (30, pp. 420-24).

It is generally thought that intelligence, seen as the capacity to learn or the ability to profit from experience, ceases to increase sometime after the end of the developmental period. Studies are inconclusive on this point; however, probably the steady year by year growth lessens in magnitude by the end of the teens, continues to increase very silghtly during the twenties, holds relatively constant during the thirties and forties, and starts decreasing slightly during the fifties. This is a very difficult statement to prove or defend, because actual experience provides so much increased stimulation and material for learning throughout middle age that isolating a factor of *ability to learn* is most difficult. By analogy with other phases of growth and the relative constancy of such standardized test scores as we have, these statements describe our current understanding. Further research is needed on growth rates in adults and on the details of differential growth rates for different levels of intelligence.

OTHER ASPECTS OF INTELLIGENCE TESTING

In describing the assessment of intelligence so far, we have dealt only with the individual test of the Binet type. These tests are given to individuals by a qualified person trained in the techniques of administration and interpretation. There are other similar tests that give the same kind of results. For practical purposes in schools, vocations, and mass research, the individual test is both too time consuming and too expensive. Much of our data on intelligence comes from standardized tests, which are administered to groups of persons and which use techniques that require less highly trained personnel. These are commonly referred to as group intelligence tests. The IQ's in typical school records are much more likely to be based upon such a testing procedure than upon the individual test, except for occasional problem cases that need more careful diagnosis. By and large, group tests are adequate and extremely useful. However, they are not as accurate or as reliable as an individual test; and they do not present as complete a clinical diagnosis as can be obtained by a clinician with an individual test.

Most group tests are pencil and paper tests that require the individual to respond to printed instructions supplemented by the general directions of the test administrator. The majority of such tests depend heavily upon language ability and present few opportunities for responses independent of language. This is justifiable, in that it was early noted that the language (especially vocabulary) phases of the individual tests correlated more highly with the total test than any other phase. A quick check of intelligence can be readily made through an appropriate vocabularly test. However, it is clear that someone with a specific language disability may not demonstrate his proficiencies as well in a group test as he might in an individual test. Motivation and other extraneous factors can also affect the results of group tests more than they would the results of individual tests. In tests that have a speed factor, important as it is, results may reflect extremes in individual rates of operations more than is justified in the total score. Good schools and good psychological studies will use group tests with awareness of their limitations and will follow up with individual checks when evidence indicates that the scores are suspect. It is common practice today to give several tests during the period of schooling in order to find typical performance and take potential errors into account.

Several group and individual tests, which emphasize performance and minimize language abilities, have been developed for special purposes. With care, it is possible to make fairly precise statements about intelligence, even for persons who deviate from the usual patterns.

Pencil and paper group intelligence tests are frequently confused by students and others with achievement tests. Technically, they are very different. Tests of academic achievement deal with information and skills that *have had* to be learned. They generally presuppose instruction in the material dealt with. Such material goes beyond immediate experience and theoretically has required specific study of some sort to master it. The intelligence test, in school use a test of academic *aptitude*, presumably tests abilities that have not been specifically taught but have been sharpened on everyday experiences available to everyone. The degree to which one demonstrates his gain from such everyday experience is taken as a prediction of his ability to learn.

The Binet type tests and many group tests give a single mental-age score and/or a derived IQ score. The statements about intelligence are global, expressed in a single figure. We can conceive of intelligence not as a single ability but as a composite of a number of separate, but perhaps related abilities. Tests that operate in this way can be more diagnostic, indicating not only that learning will be difficult or easy at a particular level for an individual, but that it will be easy or diffcult in particular ways or for particular kinds of materials.

Thurstone and others have developed the concept of primary mental abilities and have defined these through complicated statistical analyses of test performances. These abilities, taken together, are seen as a composite picture of intelligence. There are several ways of defining these abilities. One formulation lists eight primary factors (31, p. 396).

1. The space factor or the ability to visualize objects in space
2. The number factor or the ability to carry out simple arithmetical operations
3. The verbal comprehension factor
4. The word fluency factor

5. The memory factor
6. The induction factor or the ability to derive or discover a principle from a series of details or problems
7. The deduction factor or the ability to apply a principle to a series of specifics
8. Flexibility and speed in dealing with situations or problems

Thus, an individual may be superior (as compared to his age group) in several of these factors and average or low on others. His over-all performance reflects this composite. Another individual may be generally superior, with a specific weakness in one of the abilities. Whether or not these are *the* primary abilities, the concept is useful, and tests based on it can be used more diagnostically for teaching purposes than those giving a single score.

INTELLIGENCE

The question raised in the first part of this chapter has not yet been answered in final terms, but some of the concepts that point toward an answer have been clarified. In psychological literature and for practical purposes, intelligence is a quality of behavior described by the results of intelligence tests. This is a somewhat circular definition, yet it is a useful one if we recognize that such results enable us to say things about intelligence and to more readily manipulate some of the concepts involved. We must further recognize that intelligence, however defined, is only one aspect of development; and in everyday use, it carries more freight than it should bear. The more limited definition may be more realisitc in deflating some of the emotionalized value of the word.

159

IMPLICATIONS OF THE DISTRIBUTION OF INTELLIGENCE

Accepting this more limited definition, we can look at the distribution of intelligence in the general population and consider some of its implications for schooling and living.

Many features of nature and of human development may be measured and found to be distributed according to a particular pattern. Statistical analysis has given us one such pattern, the bell shaped curve of normal probability, which is extremely useful for ordering our knowledge about many facets of development. If many measures are taken of a characteristic, the greatest number of them will cluster around an average. There will be relatively fewer at the upper and lower extremes. Interestingly enough, the proportions of such a distribution of frequencies of occurrence has been so well established in actual measurements that the resulting curve can be used as a predictor of measurements yet unmade. So it is with IQ measurements, partly because of the characteristics of intelligence as such, partly because of the construction of IQ tests. The curve presented here is a thoretical one, an example of normal distribution. In actual studies with large enough populations, the actual curve approximates the one on p. 160.

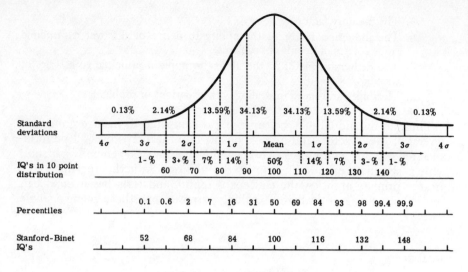

NORMAL CURVE

Any standard text on statistics will give detailed information on the normal curve and probability. For our purposes, it is enough to note the proportions of the curve that cover certain ranges of intelligence. The most useful statistical device for dividing the curve is a measure known as the "standard deviation," which points off certain distances on the base line and divides the curve into segments.

It will be noticed that the Stanford-Binet test has a standard deviation of sixteen points. Thus, approximately 34 per cent of the population falls between the IQ points of 84 and 100, the same per cent falls between 100 and 116. As we move into the lower frequency area of the curve, approximately 14 per cent falls between 68 and 84; and the same per cent falls between 116 and 132. Less than 3 per cent fall below 68 or above 132.

For practical purposes, it has become customary to think of IQ distribution in ten point divisions. These have been indicated on the curve. Since an IQ of 100 is necessarily the mean, by the very definition of IQ as the 1 to 1 relationship obtained by labelling mental age as that test performance most characteristic of an age group, this value falls at the center of the curve. By striking off equal distances along the base line, each representing ten points of IQ, we find some predictable relationships.

Fifty per cent of the normal population will fall between the IQ points of 90 and 110. This portion is commonly thought of as the "normal" IQ or the average segment. Obviously, 25 per cent will fall below 90 and the remaining 25 per cent above 110. Approximately 14 per cent will have IQ's between 80 and 90, and the same number between 110 and 120. Between 70 and 80 and between 120 and 130, approximately 7 per cent will be found in each segment.

Below 70 and above 130 will be found a very small proportion of the population. Slightly more than 3 per cent will fall between 60 and 70, and the same number between 130 and 140. Less than 1 per cent will have IQ's below 60 or above 140. Although the curve shown here extends beyond 150, it is drawn as still open. In a large enough population, there will be a few persons (one in a million) with IQ's of 180 or higher. Above this level, the assignment of specific IQ numbers is speculative, because our tests are not powerful enough to permit accuracy of statements concerning IQ's of 200 or above. Equivalent scores at the lower end of the scale are equally meaningless. Actually, those at the extreme low end seldom live into adulthood; they are too severely handicapped to adapt to the demands of living, even with institutional care.

The terminology applied to different levels of intelligence is not yet standardized. Recent literature seems to favor terminology that emphasizes the training or educational possibilities, rather than the emotionally colored labels previously in use (4, 30, p. 404).

The group with IQ's of 25 and below are being referred to as "mentally deficient: untrainable." Traditional labels for this group are "idiot," "severely retarded," "mentally defective." Those with IQ's between 25 or 30 to 50 or 60 are referred to as "mentally deficient: trainable." Common terms for this group are "imbecile" and "mentally defective." Those with IQ's between 50 or 60 to 75 or 85 are considered "educable mentally handicapped." Terms such as "moron," "feeble-minded," and "mentally retarded" have been applied to this group.

These classifications are deliberately overlapping, because diagnosis of the level of difficulty or capability requires more than an IQ rating. The terminology should be used cautiously, with no absolute or final connotation. For individuals with IQ's between about 75 to 90, the term "slow learner" is applicable; sometimes the reference is "dull" or "dull normal." An IQ of from 90 to 110 is considered normal or average. An IQ between 110 to 120 is thought of as indicating above average intelligence or, in some classifications, "superior" intelligence. For IQ's between 120 and 140, the classification "very superior" is sometimes used. The term "intellectually gifted" is frequently applied to those with IQ's above 130, while "near genius" or "genius" is sometimes used for those with IQ's above 140.

Variations in this terminology and the IQ points used for division will be found throughout the literature. It is probably wise to avoid these labels, except in very general discussions, and to apply more precise descriptions in dealing with individuals or in working with technical information. Since the IQ is a precise measure only if carefully defined, it is probably wise to think of an individual IQ as encompassing a range rather than as being an exact point on the scale. Some psychologists suggest that an IQ statement should be thought of as including plus or minus six points. For most of us, it is probably easier to think in a ten point range, so that an IQ of 105 may be thought of as falling between 100 and 110. In looking at data for large populations, such variations balance out. The curve and its segments as described in this chapter apply to such populations.

Further implications of the curve of distribution. Because of selective factors, segments of the population do not fit the normal curve. The students in a typical suburban school system are likely to have a mean

IQ of 110 or higher, because of selective factors determining the choice of residence. A population of college graduates will probably have a mean IQ of 120 or higher, and the IQ ratings will probably not go below 105. Yet, an understanding of the curve combined with an understanding of other factors permits many useful predictions. A school system setting up a special program for gifted children would need to analyze its own population, but it could make preliminary guesses based on the normal distribution. If an IQ of 130 is used as the bottom cut-off point, a high school with a student population of 500 would probably have a minimum of 20 students in such a group (500 x 4 per cent). In a particularly favored community, this number might be doubled. A school system would probably have no more than 10 such students in any one class unless it was a highly selective school, which restricted enrollment in terms of intelligence. On the other hand, if the school wished to lower its cut-off point to 120, it would have three times the number of students to select from.

It becomes apparent that a college population is "abnormal," in that colleges select students from the upper half of the IQ range. Seldom do individuals with IQ's below 110 graduate from a four year college or university. Thus, colleges, as defined and operated today, can deal with a maximum of 25 per cent of the total population.

FACTORS INFLUENCING INTELLIGENCE

By treating intelligence developmentally in following the Binet model and by operationally defining intelligence as the IQ designation derived from test performance, questions of the causation of differing levels of intelligence have been avoided. If intelligence is a term applied to the effectiveness or efficiency with which one functions, it becomes clear that, like other phases of development, intelligent behavior is caused by the interaction of native equipment with environmental pressures and opportunities.

It was emphasized in the discussion of genetic inheritance that the only inherited factor is the cellular blueprint for physical structure. Only to the extent that physical structure determines functioning is behavior inherited. Until we know more about how the structure of the brain, nervous system, and associated bodily systems governs the functioning of behaviors we call "intelligent," it is useless to speculate on the inheritance of a quality called intelligence.

Certainly, it is common sense to realize that the quality of the entire organism, in structure and physiological functioning—including the brain and nervous system—limits and sets some kind of potential for intelligent functioning. Beyond that, the stimulation of environment permits varied levels of functioning with equivalent equipment. Certainly, some of the factors commonly thought of as related to intelligence involve learning. Discrimination in perception, concept formation, language learning, and ability to manipulate objects have already been dealt with as developmental processes involving both maturation and learning.

If we think of intelligence as a way of describing a phase of the total personality, we should expect intelligence to develop in much the same way as the total personality. If the analysis of development through psychosexual stages is correct, principles applicable to the development of ego and self should apply to intelligence. As the self stabilizes, so should intelligence. We should expect more variation in an individual's intellectual performance in the early developmental years and less variation after five or six when the total personality is basically formed. IQ, as an operational analog of intellectual efficiency, should become increasingly stable along with the basic personality. Research on change and constancy of the IQ may be interpreted to support this view.

CONSTANCY OF THE IQ

Studies of change and constancy in the intelligence level are extremely difficult to interpret, because it is never clear which results are to be attributed to weaknesses in the tests and testing procedures and which should be ascribed to actual changes in the typical behavior of the subjects. With this in mind, the following interpretations are made cautiously.

A number of studies indicate individual changes in IQ of as much as 50 points between preschool ages and the age of 18 (30, pp. 410-46). In one longitudinal study, almost 10 per cent of the group changed at least 30 points over the period of time from age six to age 18. Thirty per cent changed 20 or more points (this includes those above 10 per cent) and more than 50 per cent changed by 15 or more points. In some cases, the change represented a gain, in others a loss. These statements should not obscure the fact that almost 50 per cent remained relatively constant. More careful study of individual cases indicates that some of the changes reflect life events, which could well result in depressed functioning in both testing situations and general behavior. In other cases, no such influences are apparent. In defense of constancy, the older the child, the better the prediction of his next testing; and the shorter the time between testing, the less the change. In other words, a test score made at age sixteen is a better predictor of eighteen-year-old performance than is a score made at age fourteen.

163

Similar longitudinal studies concentrating on children who showed consistent increases in IQ throughout the school years and on others who showed consistent decreases, identified personality variables and parental attitudes that were associated with these changes (26, 30, pp. 442-44). The relationship is complex and sometimes subtle, but generally children with a rising IQ were likely to have parents who encouraged emotional independence and curiosity and permitted normally aggressive behavior. The children tended to show more initiative and to be more competitive, achievement motivated, and aggressive. They were also characterized by behavior referred to as "learning how to learn." The children with dropping IQ's showed the reverse of these trends.

Cross-sectional studies of persons in "impoverished" environments yield results pointing in a similar direction. Small populations, relatively isolated from the mainstream of culture, with extremely limited opportunities for schooling or other intellectual stimulation have been found to have a lower mean IQ in older than in younger groups. The general picture of functioning seems to diminish from year to year.

A corollary to this is found in attempts with institutionalized orphan children, whose background has been impoverished and nonstimulating, to provide an extremely rich and stimulating preschool program. In some such studies, the increase in IQ is phenomenal. There is some evidence that this change proves to be relatively permanent. On the other hand, similar attempts at massive enrichment have had less effect on children from average background or on older children, perhaps indicating support of the hypothesis that the development of the basic mode of intellectual functioning runs parallel to basic personality development.

It will be recalled that the basic theory of intelligence tests is founded upon the assumption that the test content is based upon situations that *all* children have had an equal chance to encounter. When this assumption is not true, the individual's performance is not a function of his ability, but of a weakness in the test. This notion can be used to interpret some aspects of all studies of change in IQ. It has been specifically tested in research on "culturally fair" tests. Working on the premise that most intelligence tests have been developed by people from middle-class backgrounds on assumptions of standard experiences of middle-class children, attempts have been made to base test items, which test the same behavioral processes, on probable experiences of lower-class children. Vocabulary and language items have been most vulnerable to this attack. Enough has been done along this line to indicate the fact that cultural bias does exist in standard intelligence tests and that revisions of items can produce changes in results. At one time, the term "culture free" was used in such attempts. It is now generally agreed that any test must be imbedded in some cultural context. Careful attention to items may produce tests that are more culturally fair, but the tests cannot be "culture-free." In practice, where tests are used primarily for prediction of scholastic or academic achievement, cultural bias is built into school practices and prescriptions of intellectual and other developmental tasks. For special purposes and detailed diagnostic studies, "culturally fair" tests are useful; however, as yet, they cannot replace standard intelligence tests.

SUMMARY OF CHANGE AND CONSTANCY IN INTELLIGENCE

There is clear evidence of both constancy and change in the quality of functioning we call "intelligence." It appears that there is an organic and hereditary base in such functioning. We do not know the exact nature of this base; however, beyond it, the interaction of the organism and its environment provides a level of functioning that eventually becomes characteristic of the particular individual. Intelligence, like other aspects of personality, is more labile in the early developmental periods. After the onset of latency, basic change becomes more difficult. Basic personality characteristics provide the base for constancy or characteristic increase or decrease in intellectual ability.

Evidences of change in IQ are partly the result of changes in test performance as such, whether because of test weaknesses or because of temporary conditions in the life of the subject being tested. Such evidences may also indicate true change in intellectual functioning. By and large, IQ tends to be relatively constant after the early developmental periods. Variations from this constancy provide a signal for diagnosis.

Most IQ tests show some cultural bias. Depending upon the use of the tests, this bias may be valuable or damaging. The IQ test should never be used as the exclusive instrument for assessing the present abilities or future potential of an individual.

One further point has not been made explicit in the preceding text, but it should be clear as a common-sense idea. An individual performing on a test may not do as well as his potential, but he cannot do better than his potential. In other words, an individual's best performance on an intelligence test is more likely to reflect his true intelligence, assuming that testing conditions are appropriate and that there are no errors in the administration.

With a clear concept of these problems, limitations, and values, intelligence testing becomes a valuable tool for psychological understanding of individuals.

SOME LIMITATIONS OF CURRENT CONCEPTS OF INTELLIGENCE

Much has been learned over the past half-century about the psychological functioning of individuals. A significant portion of this has come from intelligence testing. During this time, the meaning of the word "intelligence," the procedures for assessing it, and the literature communicating findings and conclusions about it have crystallized. These crystallizations are reflected in the preceding discussion. Much discussion among the uninformed wishes to give different and more expanded meaning to the term "intelligence." It may be useful to resist this and to restrict this term operationally to the kinds of behavior defined by intelligence tests and expressed by IQ statements. The other viable alternative is to retain the IQ statement to refer to traditional concepts and to permit the concept of "intelligence" to expand.

In the case of either alternative, there is no implication that intelligence, as traditionally defined, or IQ data to date has attempted to talk about *all* aspects of mental behavior. Recent statistical analyses and theoretical speculations recognize that there are important kinds of functions that are apparently intellectual that could be called "intelligent," which are not typically represented in standard intelligence tests or in the bulk of the literature on intelligence. Looming large among these phases is the area commonly referred to as creative thinking or creativity (14, 16, 31, 32).

CONVERGENT THINKING, DIVERGENT THINKING, AND CREATIVITY

The very nature of IQ tests as developed recognizes the *correct* answer, the *common* answer, and the answer *typical* of the majority of an age group or a defined population. Traditional intelligence testing makes little provision for the *unusual* response, for *variety* of responses, or for *many* responses. Yet, certainly, these possibilities are phases of intellectual functioning.

Guilford and others have attempted to expand and clarify the range of intellectual functions through theoretical and statistical analysis. Among the formulated conceptions, one closely related to school practices that has generated much research and discussion is the distinction between convergent and divergent thinking (14, 16, 18, 31, 32).

Convergent thinking refers to abilities that permit us to narrow down, to focus, to limit our thinking, to give the *correct* response, the carefully defined answer, or the limited statement, which fits a carefully defined situation. This kind of thinking is usually well represented in traditional intelligence tests.

Less well represented are the divergent thinking abilities, those that open up a situation and expand or broaden thinking to original responses, unusual answers, or fluency of ideas. In areas where there are no final answers, where problem solution requires exploration of an open system rather than analysis of a closed situation, divergent abilities are thought to be most useful. It would appear that creativity—creative thinking or creative production—calls more upon the divergent than the convergent modes.

In creativity in science and art, similar abilities seem to be called for. Loewenfeld's work in analyzing creativity in art independently paralleled Guilford's work in science and came up with the following attributes of creativity. It will be noticed that some of these are checked by the usual intelligence test, others are not (18).

1. *Sensitivity to problems.* This implies insight into problem situations and the ability to perceive possibilities of their solution. Sensitivity to the significant materials or elements of the situation that may lead to solution is also included.

2. *Fluency of ideas.* The more creative person tends to have more ideas or more ways of tackling a problem or responding to a situation than the less creative.

3. *Flexibility.* This implies the ability to adapt or change quickly in new situations, to be able to shift from one approach to another, to not be bound by a few stereotyped approaches.

4. *Originality.* The uncommon response is more characteristic of the creative person than is reliance on the conventional or conforming response.

5. *Redefinition and the ability to rearrange.* This refers to the ability to see objects as potentially fulfilling functions different from the usual and to use them in a new way. There may be "nothing new under the sun," but new uses of old things is the history of expanding technology.

6. *Analysis or the ability to abstract.* This implies the ability to differentiate, to discover details, to take a situation apart in its significant parts and meanings.

7. *Synthesis and closure.* In a sense this is the opposite of analysis. In synthesis, formerly unrelated parts or elements are put together into a new whole. The closure aspect implies some foresight of how the parts or elements will go together even before the details have been worked out.

8. *Coherence of organization.* This is the ability to organize things harmoniously, so that they fit together economically. Disparate elements

are reshaped or eliminated, so that the final organization is recognized as consistent and belonging together.

If these divergent abilities are the attributes of creativity, it is clear that the creative aspects of intelligence are not coherently organized in the usual IQ tests. This statement has been tested by a number of investigations comparing children's and adolescents' tests of creativity, IQ, and achievement in school. Although there are varied details in these studies, the general conclusions seem to be consistent: IQ and creativity as tested show different distributions. Those with high IQ's are not necessarily the highly creative. Achievement in school is frequently better predicted by a combiniation of IQ and creativity scores than it is by IQ alone. Exact figures would be premature at this stage of the investigations, but it seems generally true that the peak of creativity is found in individuals with IQ's around 120. Above 130, pupils, on the average, did not display greater creativity. Those pupils with IQ's between 120 and 130, who also show high creativity, are likely to achieve as well as those with higher IQ's; in the general sense, they may be more "gifted." Most of the research on creativity has been done with persons who are average or better in IQ. It is suspected that at the IQ ranges below average, creativity will also tend to be below average.

There is some evidence that the highly creative learn better and more easily in a more fluid problem-solving situation. Memorization, rote learning, and conventional information giving are not as appropriate modes of teaching and learning for them as they may be for those high in convergent but low in divergent abilities.

There should be many implications for changes in teaching over the next decade as a result of comparative research on creativity and IQ.

THE TEACHING PROCESS

The consideration of intelligence and the additional "faces of intellect" as a phase of the development of the learner brings us back full circle to the teaching process.

Having surveyed some analyses of the learner's characteristics and some of the ways of looking at learning, how can we characterize the teacher's job?

The teacher directs and guides the learning process. He may be helped by a deeper understanding of that process, of those who undergo it, and of the potentialities of his own behavior.

A statement from a student, quoted in Chapter 1, is no more complete in itself than it was originally. Perhaps, as a result of thinking about some of the psychological perspectives, it may now have more depth:

> There is no adequate definition of teaching; however, it does encompass the following ideas: leading youngsters to develop a desire to learn; having a dedication to learning and passing this on; being aware of the needs of children and helping them grow in meeting these needs; being able

to know where to turn for concrete information and how to communicate this in an effective manner; and acting as a catalyst in developing ideas.

It encompasses this and much more.

BIBLIOGRAPHY

1. BRILL, A. A., tr. and ed., *The Basic Writings of Sigmund Freud*. New York: Modern Library Inc., Random House, 1938. Cited in Part Two, this reference is repeated for its value in explicating the theory of psychosexual stages.

2. CHURCH, JOSEPH, *Language and the Discovery of Reality*. New York: Random House, 1961. Excellent material on preverbal experience and the organizing of reality into language patterns.

3. COLEMAN, JAMES S., *The Adólescent Society*. New York: Free Press of Glencoe, Inc., 1961. A sociological study of high-school youth. Emphasizes the importance of athletics and social activities in giving status to adolescents. Raises some serious questions about the separation of adult and adolescent society.

4. CRUICKSHANK, WILLIAM M., "The Mentally Retarded Child in School," in *Freeing Capacity to Learn*, Association for Supervision and Curriculum Development, Washington, D.C.: National Education Association, 1960.

5. "DNA'S CODE: Key to all life," *Life*, LV, No. 14 (October 4, 1963), 70-90. An excellent description and visualization of the workings of the basic genetic processes.

6. DOLLARD, JOHN AND NEAL E. MILLER, *Personality and Psychotherapy*. New York: McGraw-Hill Book Company, 1950.

7. DOLLARD, JOHN et al., *Frustration and Aggression*. New Haven, Conn.: Yale University Press, 1939.

8. ENGLISH, O. SPURGEON AND GERALD H. J. PEARSON, *Common Neuroses of Children and Adults*. New York: W. W. Norton & Company, Inc., 1937.

9. ———, *Emotional Problems of Living*. New York: W. W. Norton & Company, Inc., 1945. These two books by English and Pearson outline the concept of psychosexual stages in a nontechnical way.

10. GESELL, ARNOLD et al., *The Child from Five to Ten*. New York: Harper & Row, Publishers, 1946.

11. ———, *The First Five Years of Life*. New York: Harper & Row, Publishers, 1940.

12. ———, *Infant and Child in the Culture of Today*. New York: Harper & Row, Publishers, 1943.

13. ———, *Youth, The Years from Ten to Sixteen*. New York: Harper & Row, Publishers, 1956.

14. GETZELS, JACOB W. AND PHILIP W. JACKSON, *Creativity and Intelligence*. New York: John Wiley & Sons, Inc., 1962.

15. GRINDER, ROBERT E., ed., *Studies in Adolescence*. New York: The Macmillan Company, 1963. A book of readings emphasizing research reports and theoretical considerations. Especially applicable to questions of the dynamics of identification are the papers by Burton and Whiting; McCord, McCord, and Thurber; and Peck. The description of physical growth by Tanner (pp. 417-32) was consulted for the section on physical growth in adolescence in this volume.

16. GUILFORD, J. P., "Three Faces of Intellect," *The American Psychologist*, August, 1959. Also reproduced in Crow and Crow, *Readings in Child and Adolescent Psychology*, pp. 219-37. New York: David McKay Co., Inc., 1961.

17. HAVIGHURST, ROBERT J., *Human Development and Education*. New York: David McKay Co., Inc., 1953. The lists of developmental tasks in this volume follow Havinghurst's analysis. Quotations are by permission of the publishers.

17A. ———, *Developmental Tasks and Education*, second edition, New York: David McKay Co., Inc., 1952.

18. LOEWENFELD, VIKTOR, "Current Research on Creativity," *NEA Journal*, XLVII, No. 8 (November 1958), 538-40. A similar statement appears in the Eleventh Yearbook of the American Association of Colleges for Teacher Education, 1958.

19. MASLOW, ABRAHAM H., *Motivation and Personality*. New York: Harper & Row, Publishers, 1954.

20. MONTAGU, ASHLEY, *Human Heredity*. New York: The New American Library, 1960. A paperback edition that provides the layman with much of the recent information on genetics and related aspects of development. Details of genetics presented in this volume have been checked against Montagu.

21. MULLAHY, PATRICK, *Oedipus, Myth and Complex*. New York: Hermitage Press, Inc., 1948. Analyzes various psychoanalytical treatments of the Oedipus complex and includes Sophocles' *Oedipus* trilogy.

22. NATIONAL SOCIETY FOR THE STUDY OF EDUCATION, *Mental Health in Modern Education*, Fifty-fourth Yearbook, Part II. Chicago: University of Chicago Press, 1955.

23. ———, *Child Psychology*, Sixty-second Yearbook, Part I. Chicago: University of Chicago Press, 1963.

24. RATHS, LOUIS E., *An Application to Education of the Needs Theory*. Bronxville, N.Y.: Modern Education Service, 1949. See also Raths, *The Journal of Educational Sociology*, XXIV, No. 7 (March 1951), which presents studies of the results of work with the needs theory.

25. SMITH, ROBERT PAUL, *"Where did you go?" "Out." "What did you do?" "Nothing."* New York: Pocket Books, Inc., 1957. A popular book which takes a nostalgic look at the author's own boyhood and compares it with his perception of children in the 1950's. Gives some insights into the child society and its activities.

26. SONTAG, L. W., C. T. BAKER, AND V. L. NELSON, "Mental Growth and Personality Development: a Longitudinal Study," *Monographs, Society for Research in Child Development*, XXIII, No. 2 (1958).

27. STONE, JOSEPH L. AND JOSEPH CHURCH, *Childhood and Adolescence*. New York: Random House, 1956. An easily read text that is especially helpful in its treatment of heredity, the prenatal period, and early childhood.

28. TERMAN, LEWIS M. *et al.*, *Genetic Studies of Genius: I, Mental and Physical Traits of a Thousand Gifted Children*. Stanford, Calif.: Stanford University Press, 1925.

29. TERMAN, LEWIS M. AND M. A. MERRILL, *Measuring Intelligence*. Boston: Houghton Mifflin Company, 1937. The analyses of test performances in Chapter 14 are based on the directions given in this manual. This reference should be examined to get the flavor of individual intelligence testing.

169

30. THOMPSON, GEORGE G., *Child Psychology*, second ed. Boston: Houghton Mifflin Company, 1962. An extremely useful text, especially as a reference work for presentation and interpretation of research findings. For reference to this volume, the section on intelligence (pp. 393-456) is very helpful.

31. TORRANCE, E. PAUL, "Creative Thinking of Children," *The Journal of Teacher Education*, XIII, No. 4 (December 1962).

32. ———, *Guiding Creative Talent*. Englewood Cliffs, N. J.: Prentice-Hall, Inc., 1962.

33. WATSON, ROBERT I., *Psychology of the Child: Personal, Social, and Disturbed Child Development*. New York: John Wiley & Sons, Inc., 1959. A very helpful selection is represented in Crow and Crow, *Readings in Child and Adolescent Psychology*, pp. 69-72, cited above. Our discussion of the sequence of prenatal development follows Watson's outline.

171

INDEX

173